Policy Update

for

DiNitto

Social Welfare
Politics and Public Policy

Fifth Edition

prepared by

Linda K. Cummins
Windmill Technologies

PEARSON

Boston   New York   San Francisco
Mexico City   Montreal   Toronto   London   Madrid   Munich   Paris
Hong Kong   Singapore   Tokyo   Cape Town   Sydney

Contents

Integrating Grid
Preface

Section	Page
I. SOCIAL WELFARE IN THE GLOBAL VILLAGE	1
9/11...	1
The War on Terrorism...	3
Homeland Security..	12
War on Iraq..	15
Threats in the Global Village...............................	17
II. ELECTIONS, REFORMS, AND THE BUSH PRESIDENCY	26
Presidential Election 2000...................................	26
Election Reform...	28
The George W. Bush Presidency...........................	29
Campaign Finance Reform..................................	32
III. THE ECONOMIC STATE OF THE UNION.........	40
The Boon and Bust Economy..............................	40
Boosting the Sluggish Economy...........................	44
States Struggle to Balance Budgets......................	46
From Federal Surplus to Federal Deficit...............	47
The Impact of the Economy on People's Lives........	51
America's Capacity for Giving during Economic Tough Times...................................	55
IV. POVERTY, HOMELESSNESS, AND HOUSING IN THE U.S	62
Measuring Poverty...	62
Recent Changes in the Number and Rate of Poverty...	64
Risk of poverty by age............................	66
Risk of poverty by race...........................	67
Families in Poverty..	68

Section	Page
The intersection of family structure and race: Impact on poverty	70
Homelessness in the Land of Plenty	73
Homeless families	73
Substance abuse, mental illness, and homelessness	74
Ending homelessness	74
President Bush's Homeless Agenda	74
Federal homeless programs and funding levels	75
Housing for the Poor	79
Proposed changes in federal housing Programs	79
V. THE RISE IN UNEMPLOYMENT RATES AND THE EXHAUSTION OF UNEMPLOYMENT COMPENSATION INSURANCE BENEFITS	85
The 2001 Recession and the Rise in Unemployment	85
Unemployment Compensation Claims	88
Legislation Enacted to Help Struggling Workers	89
Impact of the Bush Administration's Economic Stimulus Package on Joblessness	91
Economic Outlook	92
VI. CARING FOR FAMILIES THROUGH WELFARE REFORM: HOW WELL HAS IT WORKED?	96
Welfare Reform: How Well has it Worked?	96
How Have States Structured their TANF Programs?	96
How Have States Spent their TANF Funding?	97
Child care spending	101
Other spending	103
Spending forecast	104
TANF Program Outcomes	104
The Reauthorization of TANF	108

Section	Page

VII. CARING FOR THE NATION'S NEEDY CHILDREN 115
Implementation of the Children's Health Insurance
Program... 116
Feeding our Children..................................... 117
    The food stamp program........................ 118
    WIC.. 119
    Child nutrition programs......................... 120
Child Protection and Placement.......................... 121
    Child maltreatment............................... 121
    Out of home placements......................... 121
Child Care Assistance..................................... 124
Early Childhood Education............................... 129
    The Early Childhood Initiative and Head Start 129
    Teaching homeless children..................... 129

VIII. CARING FOR THE ELDERLY 137
Social Security Old-Age and Survivors Insurance.... 137
    Pay-as-you-go system: Collection and
Distribution of funds....................................... 137
    Who relies on Social Security?................... 140
    How many people receive Social Security
Benefits?.. 141
    Estimated benefit amounts for 2003............ 142
    How sustainable is Social Security?.............. 144
Ensuring the Health of the Elderly through Medicare. 146
The High Cost of Prescription Drugs.................... 148
The High Cost of Nursing Home Care through
Medicaid.. 150
Housing Assistance for the Elderly...................... 152

Section	Page
IX. CARING FOR THE DISABLED	157
Who are the Disabled?....................................	157
Providing a Measure of Income Security...............	157
Ticket-to-Work Medicaid Buy-Ins......................	161
President Bush's New Freedom Initiative..............	163

Table of Tables

Table		Page
1.1	Legislative Responses to 9/11...................	5
1.2	Department of Homeland Security Threat Conditions...	14
2.1	Top Ten Soft Money Donor Categories.........	34
2.2	Top Ten Soft Money Donors to Republican National Party Committee....................................	34
2.3	Top Ten Soft Money Donors to Democratic National Party Committee....................................	35
2.4	Hard Money Raise by Democratic Presidential Candidates..	36
3.1	Americans Have Less Trust in Business......	45
3.2	Growth in Federal Spending 2001-2004.......	49
3.3	Change in Median Income by Race 2000-2001	53
3.4	Income Distribution by Quintile and Top 5% Selected Years--1990-2001....................	54
3.5	Charitable Giving Comparisons by Type of Contributor..	56
4.1	Poverty Thresholds by Family Size: 2002.....	63
4.2	HHS Poverty Guidelines (Effective February 7, 2003)...	64

Table		Page
4.3	Poverty Rates for Families by Race........	69
4.4	Poverty Rates by Family Type and Race (2000-2001)......................................	72
4.5	HUD McKinney-Vento Homeless Assistance Programs...................................	76
4.6	Summary of Bringing Home America Act [H.R. 2897]......................................	77
5.1	Unemployment Rates by Selected Characteristics.............................	86
5.2	States Most and Least Affected by the Recession, July 2003	88
5.3	Summary of Legislation to Help Unemployed Workers.....................	89
6.1	Combined Federal Funds in FY 1997 & 2002 & Expenditures on Non-Assistance in FY 1997 and 2002...........................	100
6.2	Changes in TANF Caseloads 1997-2003	105
7.1	Cost of Child Care for one 4-Year Old in an Urban Child Care Center Compared to Cost of College Tuition..................................	128
7.2	Funded Early Childhood Education Programs by State.......................................	131
8.1	Cost-of-Living-Adjustments for OASDI Recipients......................................	139
8.2	Retirement Earnings Test 2003...............	140
8.3	Age to Receive Full Social Security Benefits..	143

Table		Page
8.4	Estimated Benefits by Income Level and Retirement Age 2003........................	144
9.1	Disability Rate by Race......................	151
9.2	Enrollment and Income Eligibility Characteristics of 12 States with Ticket to Work Medicaid Buy-In Programs.....................................	162

Table of Figures

Figure		Page
2.1	President Bush's Approval Ratings.......................................	29
2.2	State of the Country and Economic Confidence.....................................	31
2.3	Growth of Soft Money Raised by Political Parties..	33
3.1	Public Views of Accounting Scandals......	43
3.2	Are CEOs More or Less Honest and Ethical Than Average Persons?..............................	44
3.3	Factors Contributing to the Federal Deficit (2001-2003)..	48
3.4	Comparison of Federal Growth Rate Spending 2001-2004..	50
3.5	Federal Budget Deficit/Surplus 1999-2006...	51
3.6	Median Family Income by Family Type 2000-2001..	52
3.7	Earnings Full-Time Year-Round Workers by Gender..	53
3.8	2002 Contributions by Source..	57

Figure		Page
4.1	Number of Poor and Poverty Rate: 1959 to 2001...	65
4.2	Poverty Rates by Age: 1959 to 2001.	67
4.3	Poverty Rates by Race and Hispanic Origin: 1959 to 2001......................................	68
4.4	Poverty Rates of People in Families by Family Type and Presence of Workers: 2001.........	70
5.1	Comparison Official Unemployment Rate & Unemployed + Discouraged Workers (not seasonally adjusted)........................	86
6.1	Combined Expenditures of Federal Funds and State TANF by Spending Categories in FY 1997 through the Fourth Quarter...............................	99
6.2	Combined Expenditures of Federal Funds and State TANF by Spending Categories in FY 2002 through the Fourth Quarter................................	99
6.3	Use of TANF Funds for Child Care............	102
6.4	TANF Funds Transferred to CCDF and SSBG	103
7.1	Federal Expenditures on CHIP...................	117
7.2	Number of People who used Food Stamps 1999-2004...	118
7.3	Average Food Stamp Benefit/Person/Month..	119
7.4	Federal Spending on CACFP.....................	121
7.5	Investigation by Disposition 2001...............	123
7.6	Outcome Goals for Foster Children 2001......	125
7.7	Foster Care Outcomes 1998 & 2001.............	126
8.1	Sources and Uses of Social Security Revenues in 2002...	138
8.2	Percentage of the Aged Receiving Social Security by Relative Importance of Benefits to Total Income.....	141

Figure		Page
8.3	Beneficiaries by Type............................	142
8.4	Ratio of Workers to Social Security Beneficiaries	145
8.5	Cumulative Income less Cost Based on Present Taxes and Scheduled Benefits.....................	145
8.6	Number of Medicare Beneficiaries 1970-2030...	147
8.7	Medicare Spending in Billions 1970-2008.........	147
8.8	Annual Federal Outlays for Medicaid 1980-2003..	151
9.1	Composition of SSI Recipients by Eligibility and Age 2002..	159
9.2	Average Monthly Payment for Federally Administered SSI Benefits 2002....................................	159
9.3	Type of SSI Payments 2002.........................	160
9.4	Children Receiving SSI.............................	161

INTEGRATING GRID: LOCATING WHAT YOU NEED IN THE SUPPLIMENT AND THE PRIMARY TEXT BOOK

Supplement Topic	Section Number	Page Number	Where you can find it in the Textbook
9/11	1	1	N/A
War on Terrorism	1	3	N/A
Homeland Security	1	12	N/A
War on Iraq	1	15	N/A
Threats in the Global Village	1	17	N/A
Presidential Election 2000	2	26	N/A
Election Reform	2	28	N/A
The George W. Bush Presidency	2	29	Chapter 2
Campaign Finance Reform	2	32	Chapter 1, pp. 27-29
The Boon and Bust Economy	3	40	Chapter 2, pp. 47-50
Boosting the Sluggish Economy	3	44	Chapter 2, pp. 47-50
States Struggle to Balance Budgets	3	46	N/A
From Federal Surplus to Federal Deficit	3	47	Chapter 1, pp. 14-16; Chapter 2, pp. 43-47
The Impact of the Economy on People's Income Levels	3	51	Chapter 3, p. 77
America's Capacity for Giving during Economic Tough Times	3	55	Chapter 1, pp. 21-22
Measuring Poverty	4	62	Chapter 3, pp. 67-68
Recent Changes in the Number and Rate of Poverty	4	64	Chapter 3, pp. 69-77
Families in Poverty	4	68	Chapter 3, pp. 70-72

Homelessness in the Land of Plenty	4	73	Chapter 3, pp. 85-89
President Bush's Homeless Agenda	4	74	N/A
Housing for the Poor	4	79	Chapter 3, pp. 89-93
The 2001 recession and the rise in unemployment	5	85	Chapter 4, pp. 123-125
Unemployment compensation claims	5	88	Chapter 4, pp.123-125
Legislation enacted to help struggling workers	5	89	Chapter 4, pp.126-127
Impact of the Bush Administration's Economic Stimulus Package on Joblessness	5	91	N/A
Economic Outlook	5	92	N/A
Welfare Reform: How Well Has it Worked?	6	96	Chapter 6 pp.168-207
How Have States Structured Their TANF Programs?	6	96	Chapter 6 pp. 197-207
How Have States Spent Their TANF Funding?	6	97	Chapter 6 pp. 197-207
TANF Program Outcomes	6	104	Chapter 6 pp. 197-207
The Reauthorization of TANF	6	108	N/A
Implementing the Children's Health Insurance Program	7	116	Chapter 8, p. 280
Feeding our Children	7	117	Chapter 7, pp.215-231
Child Protection and Placement	7	121	Chapter 10, pp. 337-355
Child Care Assistance	7	127	Chapter 11, pp. 370-371

Early Childhood Education	7	129	Chapter 9, pp. 300-303
Social Security Old Age Survivors Insurance	8	137	Chapter 4, pp.114-122
Ensuring Health of the Elderly through Medicare	8	146	Chapter 8, pp.256-261
High Cost of Prescription Drugs	8	148	N/A
High Cost of Nursing Home Care through Medicaid	8	150	Chapter 8, pp. 255-256; 260-261
Housing Assistance for the Elderly	8	152	N/A
Who are the Disabled?	9	157	Chapter 5 pp.133-134
Providing a Measure of Income Security	9	157	Chapter 5 pp. 134-144
Ticket to Work Medicaid Buy-Ins	9	161	N/A
President Bush's New Freedom Initiative	9	163	N/A

PREFACE

This supplement to Diane DiNitto's policy book, *Social Welfare: Politics and Public Policy,* focuses on changes in politics, public policy, and social welfare over the past 4 years (1999-2003) from the end of the Clinton administration through the first three years of the G. W. Bush administration. As we are all aware, life has changed drastically in our global and domestic affairs. Changes at home and abroad have had dramatic impacts on social and public policies that affect the social welfare of US citizens. Many new policies have emerged since the terrorists' attacks on the US on Sept. 11, 2001, that changed our world as we had come to depend on it. Many agree that life will never be the same as it was before that dreadful day. In this supplement, special attention is given to domestic and foreign events, such as 9/11, the Afghanistan war, dramatic stock market losses and global recession, and the war on Iraq, and the impact these events have had on public attitudes, and domestics and foreign policies in force today. We have not simply changed administrations over the past 4 years, the world as we know it has changed and has had dramatic implications for the social welfare of US citizens.

Updates to the social welfare policies discussed in DiNitto's 5the edition include changes that have occurred through 1) new legislation; 2) appropriations; 3) reauthorizations; 4) policy evaluations; 5) policy regulations; 6) policy administration; and, 7) policy implementation. Changes in current political and policy perspectives, the balance of political power and influences of power groups, and reform movements on the horizon are also discussed throughout this supplement. New policy areas that have emerged since the 5/e was published, and that bear heavily on social welfare policies and practices today, are also included here. These include:

- ➤ Controversies over the 2000 election;
- ➤ Campaign finance reform;
- ➤ The Bush administration's domestic and foreign policy agendas;

- ➤ The global recession and declining US economy;
- ➤ 9/11;
- ➤ The establishment of the Department of Homeland Security;
- ➤ Terrorism;
- ➤ The war in Afghanistan;
- ➤ Unilateralism and its impact on international relations;
- ➤ The crises in State budgets;
- ➤ Tax cuts during the Bush administration;
- ➤ The growing federal deficit; and,
- ➤ The War on Iraq.

The supplement is organized by policy content area and populations, and a grid is provided for instructors so that they may locate updates in policy areas by chapter for easy integration of supplement material into the policy course.

SECTION ONE

SOCIAL WELFARE IN THE GLOBAL VILLAGE

9/11

The long held sense of security and well-being taken for granted by most Americans was shattered on September 11, 2001 when the World Trade Center and the Pentagon were attacked by the terrorist organization Al-Qaeda, under the direction of Osama bin Laden, an exiled Saudi. The extent of the damage from the attacks was massive, and those who witnessed it first hand could hardly comprehend its enormity. President Bush called the attack "The Pearl Harbor of the 21st century..."[1] The demise of over 3000 airline passengers and crew members, workers in the World Trade Center and the offices of the Pentagon, and firefighters and rescue workers[2] abruptly shifted the usual focus of human service workers' concerns for the social welfare of marginal groups, to caring for the victims of the attack, helping families cope with their losses, providing supports for stabilizing communities, and helping the rest of the country absorb and process the attack on their values, constitution, and way of life. Suddenly we were at war with an invisible enemy, who had terrorist cells around the globe. Our social welfare and the American way of life as we had come to know it, was dependent not only upon our national leaders, but also upon the support and cooperation of other world leaders who would join forces with the U.S. to avenge the attacks.

Within an hour of the attacks, President Bush went on the air and announced that the U.S. had been attacked by terrorists,[3] and later would acknowledge the terrorist attacks as acts of war.[4] Intelligence officials in Washington quickly identified the signature of Osama bin Laden, and deducted that the Al-Qaeda terrorist organization was attempting to decapitate the U.S. government.[5] It was unclear whether attacks would continue, or where they would come from, or what the government's response would be. Over the next few days, what appeared to be authentic threats on the White House continued. When President Bush refused to leave the White House, Vice President Cheney was moved to an undisclosed safe location to assure that the U.S. government would

1

continue to function, should the White House come under attack.[6] On the evening of September 11, 2001, President Bush addressed the nation and set forth what was to become known as the 'Bush Doctrine'[7] when he announced that, "We will make no distinction between those who planned these acts and those who harbor them."[8] This message spoke to any nation state that harbored terrorists, but more specifically to the Taliban regime in Afghanistan, comprised of extreme Islamic fundamentalist militia, who were known to be harboring Al-Qaeda terrorists in exchange for substantial sums of money paid by bin Laden.[9] Osama bin Laden headquartered his organization and terrorists training camps in Afghanistan under the protection of the Taliban. When the Taliban refused to surrender bin Laden and his Al-Qaeda terrorists, President Bush ordered the capture and removal of the Taliban and Al-Qaeda terrorists from Afghanistan with military force. President Bush did not ask Congress for a declaration of war, but a resolution for the use of force in fighting terrorism.[10]

Black clouds of smoke hung over New York City for three days as if in mourning for its losses; and, the skies across the country were silent and free of commercial flights for three days. In the days following the attacks, family members could be viewed on the streets of New York and on TV holding up pictures of their missing loved ones, and asking anyone who would listen if they had seen them. Large public spaces, such as the Javits Convention Center, were quickly converted to staging areas for rescue workers, survivors, and family members. Families gathered and comforted each other as they waited for word about their missing loved ones. Heartbreaking stories flooded the airways as the depth and breath of this disaster began to set in.

The American public was desperate to do something in response to the vast human need seen and heard on TV... anything to make them feel like they were helping in some small way. The American Red Cross, with the encouragement and support of the president, made a public appeal for blood donations for survivors.[11] Across the country people could be found forming long lines waiting to donate blood. Others organized support teams for the rescue workers at ground zero; pulled together local coalitions that collected food and other essential goods and transported them to New York; staged candlelight vigils in every community across the country; and human service workers from around the country, including doctors, nurses, psychologists, social workers, technicians, and others, volunteered their time and skills to help the healing begin for the survivors, families of victims, communities and the country. A year later, New York, Washington, families of victims, and the country would still be struggling with recovering from the devastating losses.

Congress, too, was quick to respond to the terrorist attacks. Table 1.2 summarizes the legislation that was passed between September 11, 2001 and October 30, 2002 that was a response to 9/11. Legislation was swift to provide funds for victims and their families and money to communities to help in their recovery. Security was a primary focus, and economic support for airlines to get the nation flying again and to provide enhanced security on aircraft and in airports was appropriated by Congress. To expedite the fight against terrorism, multiple pieces of legislation provided funds for intelligence gathering, law enforcement, and new rules for preventing terrorism. And, military appropriations and authorization for use of force paved the way for routing out the Al Qaeda terrorist camps in Afghanistan, along with the Taliban regime that harbored them. Funds for food, medical supplies, educational assistance and other humanitarian aid was appropriated for the citizens of Afghanistan.[12]

The War on Terrorism

The "first bullet in the war against terrorism"[13] was the executive order issued on Sept. 24, 2001 by President Bush to freeze financial accounts of suspected supporters of the Al-Qaeda network.[14] The treasury department began freezing financial accounts of organizations known to be used to move and collect money for terrorist networks. Often these were non-government associations, such as charity organizations. The Al-Qaeda financial network spanned the globe,[15] and Washington put pressure on international coalition members to follow suit in their respective countries. As a show of global support, the United Nations Security Council passed a resolution proposed by the U.S. that called on its member countries to break ties with terrorist groups and to freeze assets.[16] By November, 2002, 167 countries were blocking terrorist assets, and $113.5 million in terrorist assets had been frozen worldwide.[17]

3

By October, 2001, the White House had devised a military response to the 9/11 attacks that included the CIA, U.S. military Special Forces, and the arming of 20,000 Northern Alliance resistant fighters in Afghanistan.[18] This three part response was supported by a coalition of 35 plus countries from around the world who rallied behind the U.S., shaking their fists at global terrorism.[19] Secretary of State Colin Powell's statement, It's [terrorism] a scourge, not only against the United States, but against civilization, and it must be brought to an end."[20] resonated with the coalition of allies and defenders of democracy. Following suite, NATO passed a resolution invoking article 5 that declared the attacks on the U.S. an attack on all NATO countries.[21] By November, 2002, over 90 countries would join the coalition against terrorism.[22]

Table 1.1: Legislative Responses to 9/11

Legislation	Content	Signed Into Law
Benefits to Victims:		
Public Safety Officer Benefits Act (H.R. 2882)	Provided for the expedited payment of certain benefits for public safety officers who were killed or suffered a catastrophic injury in the line of duty in connection with the terrorist attacks of September 11, 2001.	9/18/2001 Public Law No: 107-37
Victims of Terrorism Relief Act of 2001 (H.R. 2884)	Amended the Internal Revenue Code of 1986 to provide tax relief for victims of the terrorist attacks.	1/23/2002 Public Law No: 107-134
Air Transportation Safety and System Stabilization Act (H.R. 2926)	Provided compensation to airlines, and established victim compensation fund for victims of the September 11, 2001 attacks; established new standards within the aviation industry.	9/22/2001 Public Law No: 107-42
Extension of unemployment assistance under the Robert T. Stafford Disaster Relief and Emergency Assistance Act in the case of victims of the terrorist attacks. (H.R.	Directs the President to make unemployment assistance available for 39 weeks after the major disaster is declared to individuals eligible under the Robert T. Stafford Disaster Relief and Emergency Assistance Act as a	3/25/2002 Public Law No: 107-154

3986)	result of the terrorist attacks of September 11, 2001.	
Mychal Judge Police and Fire Chaplains Public Safety Officers' Benefit Act of 2002 (S 2431)	Amended the Omnibus Crime Control and Safe Streets Act of 1968 to ensure that chaplains killed in the line of duty receive public safety officer death benefits.	6/24/2002 Public Law No: 107-196
Community Recovery and Public Safety:		
2001 Emergency Supplemental Appropriations Act for Recovery from and Response to Terrorist Attacks on the United States (H.R. 2888)	Made emergency supplemental appropriations for the fiscal year 2001 for additional disaster assistance, for anti-terrorism initiatives, and for assistance in the recovery from the tragedy that occurred on September 11, 2001.	9/18/2001 Public Law No: 107-38
Bioterrorism Response Act of 2001 (H.R. 3448)	Improves the ability of the United States to prevent, prepare for, and respond to bioterrorism and other public health emergencies.	6/12/2002 Public Law No: 107-188
Transportation Security		
Air Transportation Safety and System Stabilization Act	Provided compensation to airlines, and established victim compensation fund	9/22/2001 Public Law No:

(H.R. 2926)	for victims of the September 11, 2001 attacks; established new standards within the aviation industry.	107-42
Aviation and Transportation Security Act (S 1447)	Strengthens aviation and transportation security by establishing 1) the Transportation Security Administration, 2) the Transportation Security Oversight Board; 3) the position of Federal Security Manager in each U.S. airport to oversee the screening of passengers; and, 4) the use of Federal air marshals. Authorizes appropriations for FY 2002 through 2005 for aviation security activities; authorizes the pilot of a passenger aircraft to carry a firearm into the cockpit.	11/19/2001 Public Law No: 107-71
Strengthening Law Enforcement and Intelligence Gathering:		
Intelligence Authorization Act for Fiscal Year 2002 (H.R. 2883)	Authorized appropriations for fiscal year 2002 for intelligence and intelligence-related activities.	12/28/2001 Public Law No: 107-108
Uniting and Strengthening	Enhances law enforcement	10/26/2001

America by Providing Appropriate Tools Required to Intercept and Obstruct Terrorism (USA PATRIOT ACT) act of 2001 (H.R. 3162)	investigatory tools in order to deter and punish terrorist acts in the United States and around the world	Public Law No: 107-56
Terrorist Bombings Convention Implementation Act of 2001 (H.R. 3275)	Implemented the International Convention for the Suppression of Terrorist Bombings to strengthen criminal laws relating to attacks on places of public use, to implement the International Convention of the Suppression of the Financing of Terrorism, to combat terrorism and defend the Nation against terrorist acts.	6/25/2002 Public Law No: 107-197
Protecting our Borders:		
Enhanced Border Security and Visa Entry Reform Act of 2002 (H.R. 3525)	Enhances the border security of the United States through increased appropriations for the U.S District Attorney's office and Immigration and Naturalization Service; mandating interagency information sharing; and establishing an electronic system for verifying and monitoring legal immigrants, including students.	5/14/2002 Public Law No: 107-173

A bill to amend the Immigration and Nationality Act (S 1424)	Amends the Immigration and Nationality Act to repeal the September 13, 2001, expiration of (thus granting permanent authority for) the provision of nonimmigrant "S" visas to aliens who possess, and will supply (or have supplied) to law enforcement agencies, critical information respecting criminal or terrorist organizations.	10/1/2001 Public Law No: 107-45
Military:		
National Defense Authorization Act for Fiscal Year 2002(S 1438)	Authorized appropriations for fiscal year 2002 for military activities of the Department of Defense, for military constructions, and for defense activities of the Department of Energy, to prescribe personnel strengths for such fiscal year for the Armed Forces.	12/28/2001 Public Law No: 107-107
A joint resolution expressing the sense of the Senate and House of Representatives regarding the terrorist attacks launched against the United States on September 11, 2001 (S.J. Res. 22)	Condemns the terrorists who planned and carried out the September 11, 2001 attacks against the United States, as well as their sponsors. Extends condolences to the victims and their families, friends, and loved ones. Declares that these premeditated attacks struck not only at the people of	9/18/2001 Public Law No: 107-39

	America, but also at the symbols and structures of our economic and military strength, and that the United States is entitled to respond under international law.	
Authorization for Use of Military Force (S.J. Res. 23)	A joint resolution to authorize the use of United States Armed Forces against those responsible for the recent attacks launched against the United States.	9/18/2001 Public Law No: 107-40
Humanitarian Aid:		
Afghan Women and Children Relief Act of 2001 (S 1573)	Authorized the provision of educational and health care assistance to the women and children of Afghanistan.	12/12/2001 Public Law No: 107-81
Patriot Day:		
Designating September 11 as Patriot Day (H. J. Res. 71)	Declare September 11 as Patriot Day.	12/18/2001 Public Law No: 107-89

Information gather from The Library of Congress: Thomas: Legislative Information on the Internet (last revised Oct. 30, 2002)
http://thomas.loc.gov/

As military plans against the Taliban and Al-Qaeda began to materialize, President Bush insisted that the 'first bombs' dropped in Afghanistan be humanitarian aid to the needy village people under the oppressive regime of the Taliban.[23] Since that time, the United States Government has provided $850 million for humanitarian and reconstruction assistance in Afghanistan.[24] The international community wanted to help the U.S. in its war against terrorist, and 16 countries were involved in the military campaign.[25] however, the key roles were filled by U.S. military, CIA, FBI, and the British military. By December 7, 2001, 110 CIA officers and 316 Special Forces personnel, plus massive air raids by U.S. and British military[26] and soldiers of the Northern Alliance, occupied the whole of Afghanistan, and the Taliban and Al-Qaeda operatives had fled the country. By December 22, 102 days after 9/11, a new leader supported by the Northern Alliance and leaders of neighboring countries, Hamid Karzai, was installed as the new leader in Afghanistan.[27] As of August, 2003, more than 60,000 American troops are deployed around the world against terrorism: 7,000 are stationed in Afghanistan.[28] Others are stationed in the Philippines, Soviet Republic of Georgia, and Yemen.[29] Thirty-one nations have deployed more than 14,000 troops in support of Operation Enduring Freedom in Afghanistan.[30]

The war on terrorism is far from over. Most of the 22 top Al-Qaeda leaders remain at large. Covert CIA teams as well as intelligence officers of allies rounded up thousands of suspects across the globe.[31] Attorney General John Ashcroft directed the FBI and the Justice Department to shift its focus from investigation and prosecution, to prevention.[32] Twelve hundred FBI agents were reassigned to terrorism with a focus on preempting future attacks on America, and tracking down and smoking out bin Laden supporters in the U.S. In a short time, the FBI had identified 331 suspected terrorists in the U.S. and put them on their 'watch list.'[33] To maximize the clandestine war efforts abroad, and the efforts at home, President Bush authorized unprecedented authority to the CIA and FBI. Through world-wide efforts, and the sharing of intelligence across countries, approximately 2290 terrorist-related arrests were made in 99 countries between September 12, 2001 and October 28, 2002.[34]

Homeland Security

A major step in the protection of the homeland was the establishment of a new government agency called the Department of Homeland Security (DHS), headed by Tom Ridge, former governor of Pennsylvania. This agency was authorized by the Homeland Security Act of 2002 [H.R. 5005][35] and came into being January 24, 2003. It was preceded by the President's Homeland Security Advisory Council and Senior Advisory Committees for Homeland Security established by an Executive Order March 19, 2002.[36]

The Department of Homeland Security (DHS) represents a consolidation of 22 previously distinct domestic agencies brought together for the primary purpose of protecting the nation against future terrorists' attacks on the homeland.[37] DHS is made up of 179,000 federal employees and has a budge of $36 billion.[38]

The functions within DHS include, but are not limited to: 1) analyzing threats and intelligence; 2) guarding our borders and airports; 3) protecting our critical infrastructure; and, 4) coordinating the response of our nation for future emergencies. The DHS is also dedicated to protecting citizen rights and enhancing public services in preparation for and in times of as natural disasters.[39] The 22 agencies that were subsumed under the DHS make up four major directorates. These are:

1. The Border and Transportation Security Directorate
   Responsibilities: Border security and transportation operations.
2. The Emergency Preparedness and Response Directorate
   Responsibilities: Overseeing domestic disaster preparedness training and coordinating government disaster response.
3. The Science and Technology Directorate
   Responsibilities: Exploit all scientific and technological resources for securing the homeland.
4. Information Analysis and Infrastructure Protection Directorate
   Responsibilities: Analyzes intelligence gathered from other agencies such as the CIA and FBI, to assess threats to homeland security and to evaluate vulnerabilities in the nation's infrastructure.[40]

An important function of the DHS in keeping the nation safe is to assist states and cities in developing first response teams in the event of future terrorists' attacks. DHS is responsible for awarding and overseeing grants to states, cities, and port securities for preventing, preparing and responding to terrorism. Nearly $4 billion has been made available to state and local governments to help meet the needs of first responders and to offset costs associated with extra security measures[41]

Since its inception January, 2003, DHS has also made headway in other areas of homeland defense. They have:

➢ Worked with Center for Disease Control (CDC) and other scientists to develop strategies against biological warfare;

➢ Developed programs to safeguard the nation's financial systems against criminal exploitation;[42]

➢ Initiated Operation Predator, a comprehensive program for identifying child predators and removing them from the United States (if subject to deportation); and also works to identify children depicted in child pornography to help in their rescue;[43]

➢ Created the position of Citizenship and Immigration Ombudsman, who acts as an advocate for the public and immigrants to the Department of Homeland Security for Immigration issues;[44] and,

➢ Worked with scientists in implementing new technologies for improved safety under the auspices of The Support Anti-Terrorism by Fostering Effective Technologies Act of 2002 ("SAFETY Act");[45]

Most recently, The Transportation Security Administration (TSA) under the DHS is working to develop the Computer Assisted Passenger Prescreening System, or "CAPPS II." This program will be designed to keep terrorists off commercial flights, and to identify violent criminals with outstanding federal or state arrest warrants. When active, CAPPS II will use routine information provided by passengers when making reservations to confirm a traveler's identity and assess a risk level.[46]

While the Department of Homeland Defense has accomplished much in its short existence, what has become abundantly clear is that protecting and sealing the U.S. borders is nearly impossible, even with heightened security. The U.S. remains a nation at risk for terrorists attacks.[47] To keep citizens informed of the latest levels of risk for terrorists' attacks, the DHS post the current alert levels daily on its web site at (http://www.whitehouse.gov/homeland/).[48] Threat Conditions are represented by color codes from low threat conditions (green) to severe threat conditions (red). Table 1.2 below summarizes the threat levels and coordinates them with their assigned color code.[49]

Table 1.2: Department of Homeland Security Threat Conditions

COLOR CODE	THREAT LEVEL	DESCRIPTION OF THREAT LEVEL
GREEN	LOW	Low risk of terrorist attacks.
BLUE	GUARDED	There is a general risk of terrorists' attacks. Federal departments and agencies are encouraged to review and update emergency response procedures.
YELLOW	ELEVATED	A significant risk of terrorists attacks exist. Federal departments and agencies are encouraged to increase surveillance and to implement response plans as needed.
ORANGE	HIGH	A high risk for terrorists' attacks exist. Federal departments and agencies are encouraged to coordinate security efforts with federal, state, and local law enforcement agencies; take additional precautions at public events; and to restrict threatened facility access to essential personnel.
RED	SEVERE	Severe risks of terrorists' attacks exist. Federal departments and agencies are encouraged to increase and redirect personnel to address critical emergency needs; assign emergency response personnel; monitor public transportation systems; and close government and public facilities.

Information taken from the Department of Homeland Security web page
http://www.dhs.gov/dhspublic/display?theme=9

War on Iraq

The question of Iraq and its role in world terrorism arose soon after 9/11 and members of the National Security Council (NSC) argued long and hard about whether to include Iraq in the initial assaults against terrorism.[50] Initially, the NSC decided to focus on Afghanistan, but Iraq continued to bubble on the back burner. It had long been suspected Saddam Hussein was developing weapons of mass destruction (chemical, biological, and nuclear),[51] however hard evidence supporting this position was limited and unconvincing to the international community.[52]

The response of the international community to the 9/11 attacks on the U.S. were swift and supportive, but as talk turned to war with Iraq, world leaders began to distance themselves from the U.S. Early on, allies feared that President Bush would engage in unilateralism.[53] President Bush was adamant that other countries not dictate the terms or condition of the war on terrorism,[54] and was resolute that world leaders equate their national interest with that of America's. By May 2002, the president was having difficulty getting Europe, Russia, and the Middle East to buy into his anti-terrorism vision 100%.[55] In the end, a coalition of 49 countries emerged that supported "Operation Iraqi Freedom." Most were small countries that provided public or vocal support; however, the substantive support for the US war against the president of Iraq, Saddam Hussein, was given primarily by Australia, Britain, and Spain.[56]

During his State of the Union Address on January, 29, 2002 President Bush declared Iraq, Iran, and North Korea as "an axis of evil." He altered U.S. war policy when he said "I will not wait on events," suggesting that he would act preemptively against perceived threats to the U.S.[57] In preparation for a military strike against Iraq, President Bush allocated $200 million to step up intelligence gathering in Iraq, preparation for CIA paramilitary teams, and U.S. Special Forces. By April, 2002, the president was openly advocating for a regime change in Iraq.[58]

The talk of war with Iraq put world leaders on edge, especially those in the Middle East region. Consequences were estimated to be high. Some feared that a war with Iraq could destabilize the whole region, as well as have staggering economic implications given the oil rich countries in the region. Others believed that it may prompt more terrorists' attacks, and escalate the rising resentment toward the U.S. world wide.[59] In an attempt to engage the world in addressing the perceived world threat of Saddam Hussein, President Bush used his scheduled speech to the United Nations on September 12, 2002 to call them on their lack of response to Saddam's violations of U.N. resolutions, particularly the resolutions calling for weapons inspections. Saddam kicked out U.N. weapons inspector in 1998. President Bush asked the U. N. to take action.[60] Since the U.N. acts through resolution, President Bush was, in effect, asking for a new resolution to return inspectors to Iraq. The day following President Bush's speech, Saddam Hussein announced that he would allow U.N. weapons inspectors to enter Iraq. By November, a U.N. resolution had been written and was passed unanimously by the U.N. Security Council.[61] In spite of his success at mobilizing the U.N., President began publicly pushing for military action against Saddam Hussein and his military guard. Most countries insisted that inspectors be given time to do a thorough inspection. Russia and France, permanent members of the U. N. Security Council, said that they would veto any resolution for military force against Iraq, because they did not feel that a clear and compelling case had been made against Hussein. Consequently, a second resolution calling for military force against Iraq was withdrawn by the U.S. By October 11, Congress had voted to give President Bush full authority to attack Iraq unilaterally. By December, Hussein had supplied inspectors with a 12,000 page document that denounced the accusations that Iraq had weapons of mass destruction.[62] This document proved "not enough to create confidence," according to U.N. inspectors,[63] and was declared "another material breach" of existing resolutions by Secretary of State, Colin Powell.[64]

An apparent imminent attack on Iraq by the U.S spawned antiwar protest by the millions around the world, and by the tens of thousands at home. On March 19, 2003, the U.S. went to war with Iraq with support from Britain, Spain, and Australia.[65] The stated purpose of the was to, "disarm Iraq of its weapons of mass destruction, and enforce 17 UNSC resolutions...[and to] liberate the Iraqi people from one of the worst tyrants and most brutal regimes on earth." [66] Victory was declared by U.S. and coalition forces three weeks later when the major military resistance in Baghdad fell, and was symbolized with the toppling of a statue of Saddam Hussein by U.S. Marines and Iraqi citizens.[67] Since that time, Saddam Hussein has eluded military forces, and no evidence exist that he is dead.[68] The U.S. has offered monetary rewards of $15-30 million for persons providing critical information leading to the capture or killing of Saddam Hussein and his sons.[69] In July, 2003, military forces were tipped off regarding the whereabouts of Saddam's sons, who were subsequently attack and killed by U.S. military forces.[70]

U.S. soldiers remain in Iraq as peacekeeping forces. As of this writing, August, 2003, U.S. troops continue to be attacked 12-20 times a day by resistance fighters inside Iraq.[71] President Bush has said he expects occupation to last 2 years. Despite U.S. successes in Iraq, the Center for Strategic and International Studies July, 2003 report cautioned that additional infusions of money and administrative personnel were necessary to ensure a stable and friendly Iraq. Specifically, there report called for:

- More military troops;
- A large-scale public works projects to get Iraqis employed and an infrastructure rebuilt;
- Improvement in the communication with the Iraqi people; and,
- Quickly widening the range of international allies on reconstruction.[72]

As of this writing (August, 2003), the Bush administration had decided against involving the United Nations in the occupation of Iraq, opting instead to enlist a wider coalition of countries to assist in reconstruction Iraq and bringing stability to the country. The occupation forces are made up of 139,000 US troops and 21,000 troops from 18 countries. Most of these (11,000) are from Britain. The US is currently seeking a resolution from the U.N. that would recognize the 25-member Governing Council in Iraq set up by the US and Britain and headed by L. Paul Bremer III, an American administrator, as a legitimate ruling structure.[72]

Threats in the Global Village

Since September 11, 2001, the U.S. has avoided direct attacks on its homeland; however, Americans have been the targets of terrorists' acts abroad. Resent attacks include:

- October 12 , 2002, terrorists members of the Islamic militant group Jemmah Islamiyah bombed a night club in Bali killing 202 people. "The targets were the Americans and the Jews," said Amrozi, a terrorist convicted in the attack;[74]

- August 5, 2003, a car bombing occurred at U S owned Marriott Hotel in Jakarta, Indonesia, killing 12 and wounding 150. Intelligence officers suspect it was carried out by Jemmah Islamiyah;[75]

- August 7, 2003 an attack on the Jordanian Embassy in Iraq killed 17 people and wounded 65. The attack is believed to be in protest to Jordan's support of the US presence in Iraq.[76]

- August 19, 2003 a suicide bomber drove a truck full of explosives into the United Nations headquarters in Baghdad, the capital of Iraq, killing 17 and wounding 40. This occurred at a time when the U. N. was considering a resolution for giving legitimacy to the U. S. occupancy of Iraq.[77]

Other threats have been stated publicly by "axis of evil" countries, Iran and North Korea. Iran claims to have midrange missiles that can reach up to 930 miles to its target, giving Iran access to Israel and American troops stationed in Iraq.[78] North Korea has openly threatened the U.S. with nuclear weapons. Talks are underway between the U.S. and it allies and North Korea. The group is considering offering economic benefits to North Korea in exchange for shutting down and dismantling its nuclear weapons program.[79]

The continued presence of the U S in Iraq has prompted Muslim militants to reenter Iraq and launch attacks against the occupying forces. Leaders in the region fear that Iraq may be the setting for Jihad, or the Holy War against the Americans as proclaimed by Fundamentalist Islamic terrorist groups. Jihad has such appeal for a wide range of militants that it is attracting support from foreign groups who are slipping into Iraq to form a resistance force against the occupying American and coalition forces.[80] It is expected that the war on terrorism will be demanding and lengthy.

ENDNOTES:

1. Bob Woodward, *Bush at War* (New York: Simon & Schuster), p. 37.
2. Phil Hirschkorn, CNN New York Bureau *New York adjusts terrorist death toll downward,* August 22, 2002. CNN.com./US, http://www.cnn.com/2002/US/08/22/9/11.toll/ Accessed August 7, 2003.
3. President George W. Bush, *Statement by the President in His Address to the Nation,* September 11, 2001 8:35 P.M. EST. http://www.whitehouse.gov/news/releases/2001/09/200109/11-16.html Accessed August 7, 2003.
4. President George W. Bush, *Guard and Reserves "Define Spirit of America" Remarks by the President to Employees at the Pentagon,* September 17, 2001, 11:45 A.M. EDT. http://www.whitehouse.gov/news/releases/2001/09/20010917-3.html Accessed August 8, 2003.
5. President George W. Bush, *Address to a Joint Session of Congress and the American People,* September f20, 2001, United States Capitol, Washington DC. http://www.whitehouse.gov/news/releases/2001/09/20010920-8.html Accessed August 8, 2003.
6. Bob Woodward, *Bush at War* (New York: Simon & Schuster), pp. 55-57.
7. Ibid. p. 30.
8. President George W. Bush, *Statement by the President in His Address to the Nation,* September 11, 2001 8:35 P.M. EST.

http://www.whitehouse.gov/news/releases/2001/09/200109/11-16.html Accessed August 7, 2003.

9. Bob Woodward, *Bush at War* (New York: Simon & Schuster), p. 32.

10. 107th Congress. *Joint Resolution, to authorize the use of United States armed forces against those responsible for recent attack s launched against the United States.* [DOCID: f:pub1040.107] Public Law 107-40. September 18, 2001 – [S. J. Res. 23]. http://frwebgate.access.gpo.gov/cgi-bin/getdoc.cgi?dbname=107_cong_public_laws&docid=f:publ040.107 August 8, 2003.

11. President George W. Bush, *Statement by the President in His Address to the Nation,* September 11, 2001 8:35 P.M. EST. http://www.whitehouse.gov/news/releases/2001/09/200109/11-16.html Accessed August 7, 2003.

12. The Library of Congress: *Thomas: Legislative Information on the Internet,* (last revised Oct. 30, 2002). http://thomas.loc.gov/

13. Bob Woodward, *Bush at War* (New York: Simon & Schuster), p. 120.

14. President George W. Bush, *Executive Order on Terrorist Financing: Blocking Property and Prohibiting Transactions with Person who Commit, Threaten to Commit, or Support Terrorism,* September 24, 2001, http://www.whitehouse.gov/news/releases/2001/09/20010924-1.html Accessed August 7, 2003.

15. Judith Miller with Kurt Eichenwald, "A Nation Challenged: The Investigation: U.S. Set to Widen Financial Assault," *New York Times,* October 1, 2001, p. 1.

16. Bob Woodward, *Bush at War* (New York: Simon & Schuster), p. 172.

17. U.S. Department of Homeland Security, *Fact Sheet: News About the War Against Terror*, November 16, 2002. http://www.dhs.gov/dhspublic/display?content=345, accessed August 4, 2003.

18. Bob Woodward, *Bush at War* (New York: Simon & Schuster), pp. 51-53.

19. Ibid. p. 65.

20. U.S. Department of State Secretary Colin L. Powell, *On-The-Record Briefing (1430 hrs): Remarks to the Press, Washington,*

DC, September 12, 2001,
http://www.state.gov/secretary/rm/2001/4880.htm Accessed
August 8, 2003.

21. U.S. Department of Homeland Security *News About the War
   Against Terror,*
   http://www.dhs.gov/dhspublic/display?content=345, Accessed
   August 4, 2003.

22. Bob Woodward, *Bush at War* (New York: Simon & Schuster),
   pp. 176.

23. U.S. Department of Homeland Security, *News About the War
   Against Terror,*
   http://www.dhs.gov/dhspublic/display?content=345, accessed
   August 4, 2003.

24. Bob Woodward, *Bush at War* (New York: Simon & Schuster), p.
   160.

25. U.S. Department of Homeland Security, *News About the War
   Against Terror,*
   http://www.dhs.gov/dhspublic/display?content=345, accessed
   August 4, 2003.

26. Elisabeth Bumiller, "A Nation Challenged: The White House;
   Bush Vows to Aid Other Countries in War on Terror," *New York
   Times,* March 12, 2002, p. 1

27. Patrick E. Tyler, "A Nation Challenged: The Attack; U.S. and
   Britain Strike Afghanistan, Aiming at Bases and Terrorist
   Camps: Bush Warns: Taliban will Pay a Price," *New York Times,*
   October 8, 2001, p. 1.

28. Bob Woodward, *Bush at War* (New York: Simon & Schuster),
   pp. 315.

29. Elisabeth Bumiller, "A Nation Challenged: The White House;
   Bush Vows to Aid Other Countries in War on Terror," *New York
   Times,* March 12, 2002, p. 1

30. Bob Woodward, *Bush at War* (New York: Simon & Schuster),
   pp. 339.

31. U.S. Department of Homeland Security, *Homeland Security Act
   of 2002,* http://www.dhs.gov/dhspublic/display?theme=46,
   accessed August 4, 2003.

32. Bob Woodward, *Bush at War* (New York: Simon & Schuster),
   pp. 316.

33. Ibid. p. 76.

34. Ibid. p. 117.

35. U.S. Department of Homeland Security, *Homeland Security Act of 2002,* http://www.dhs.gov/dhspublic/display?theme=46, accessed August 4, 2003.

36. Ibid.

37. President George W. Bush web pages: *Homeland Security Council Executive Order* http://www.whitehoU.S.e.gov/news/releases/2002/03/20020321-9.html, accessed August 4, 2003.

38. U.S. Budget 2004, Office of Management and Budget, February 3, 2003, p.4, http://w3.access.gpo.gov/usbudget/index.html Accessed August 24, 2003.

39. U.S. Department of Homeland Security, *DHS Organization: Building a Secure Homeland,* http://www.dhs.gov/dhspublic/theme_home1.jsp, Accessed July 29, 2003.

40. Ibid.

41. Ibid

42. U.S. Department of Homeland Security, *Fact Sheet: Department of Homeland Security Funding for States and Cities,* May 21, 2003. http://www.dhs.gov/dhspublic/display?content=755, accessed August 4, 2003.

43. U.S. Department of Homeland Security, *Fact Sheet: Operation Predator*, January 9, 2003. http://www.dhs.gov/dhspublic/display?content=1067, accessed August 4, 2003.

44. Ibid.

45. U.S. Department of Homeland Security, *Secretary of Homeland Security Tom Ridge Announces Citizenship and Immigration Ombudsman,* July 29, 2003. http://www.dhs.gov/dhspublic/display?content=1098, accessed August 4, 2003.

46. U.S. Department of Homeland Security, *Safety Act Regulations Submitted for 30-Day Public Comment Periods,* July 11, 2003. http://www.dhs.gov/dhspublic/display?content=1073, accessed August 4, 2003.

47. U.S. Department of Homeland Security, *CAPPS II Privacy Act Notice,* http://www.dhs.gov/dhspublic/display?content=1115, accessed August 4, 2003.

48. U.S. Department of Homeland Security, *Threat Advisory,* http://www.dhs.gov/dhspublic/, accessed July 29, 2003.
49. U.S. Department of Homeland Security, *Threats and Protection: Understanding the Homeland Security Advisory System,* http://www.dhs.gov/dhspublic/display?theme=29 , accessed August 4, 2003.
50. Bob Woodward, *Bush at War* (New York: Simon & Schuster), p. 329.

51. U.S. White House, *Renewal in Iraq: Special Report: Press Briefing on Iraq WMD and SOTU Speech,* July 22, 2003. http://www.whitehouse.gov/news/releases/2003/07/iraq/2003072 2-12.html Accessed August 7, 2003.
52. Michael Ratner, Jennie Green, and Barbara Olshansky of the Center for Constitutional Rights (New York: Seven Stories Press), pp. 14-19.
53. Bob Woodward, *Bush at War* (New York: Simon & Schuster), p. 44.
54. I Ibid. p. 81.
55. Ibid. p. 327.
56. U.S. White House, *Operation Iraqi Freedom, Iraq: Special Report: The Coalition.* April 3, 2003. http://www.whitehouse.gov/infocus/iraq/news/20030327- 10.html Accessed August 7, 2003.
57. President George W. Bush, *State of the Union Address,* January 29, 2002, http://www.whitehouse.gov/news/releases/2002/01/20020129- 11.html Accessed August 7, 2003.
58. Bob Woodward, *Bush at War* (New York: Simon & Schuster), pp. 329-330.
59. Ibid. p. 332.
60. President George W. Bush, *President's Remarks at the United Nations General Assembly*, September 12, 2002, http://www.whitehouse.gov/news/releases/2002/09/20020912- 1.html Accessed August 8, 2002.
61. Bob Woodward, *Bush at War* (New York: Simon & Schuster), pp. 347-353.
62. Ibid. pp. 351-355.
63. Ibid. pp. 354-357.

64. U. S. Secretary of State Colin L. Powell, *Interview on CNN's Late Edition with Wolf Blitzer*, December 29, 2002, Washington, DC. http://www.state.gov/secretary/rm/2002/16244.htm Accessed August 8, 2003.

65. Bob Woodward, *Bush at War* (New York: Simon & Schuster), pp. 354-357.

66. U.S. White House *Operation Iraqi Freedom, Iraq: Special Report: The Coalition,* April 3, 2003. http://www.whitehouse.gov/infocus/iraq/news/20030327-10.html Accessed August 7, 2003.

67. Bob Woodward, *Bush at War* (New York: Simon & Schuster), p. 357.

68. Ari Fleischer, *Press Briefing,* Washington DC, April 17, 2003. http://www.whitehouse.gov/news/releases/2003/04/20030417-8.html Accessed August 8, 2003.

69. U.S. White House *Operation Iraqi Freedom, Ira: Global Message,* August 6, 2003, http://www.whitehouse.gov/news/releases/2003/08/20030806-1.html Accessed August 12, 2003.

70. U.S. White House web pages. Renewal in Iraq, Special Report: *Press Briefing on Iraq WMD and SOTU Speech,* July 22, 2003. http://www.whitehouse.gov/news/releases/2003/07/iraq/2003072 2-12.html Accessed August 7, 2003.

71. Tony Karon, "What the Hussein Brothers' Deaths Mean for Iraq," *Time Magazine,* August 11, 2003.

72. Dr. John Hamre, Fredrik Barton, Bathsheba Crocker, Dr. Johanna Mendelson-Forman, and Dr. Robert Orr, *Iraq's Post-Conflict Reconstruction: A Field Review and Recommendations,* July 17, 2003, Washington DC: Center for Strategic and International Studies.

73. Steven R. Weisman with Felicity Barringer, "U.S. Abandons Idea of Bigger U.N. Role in Iraq Occupation," *New York Times,* August 14, 2003.

74. Jane Perlez, "Court decides to sentence Bali bomber to death." *New York Times,* August 8, 2003.

75. Associate Press, "Indonesia Arrests 9 in Deadly Hotel Blast," *New York Times,* August 18, 2003.

76. Michael R. Gordon, "New, soft targets in Iraq: Bombing shirts the focus," *New York Times,* August 8, 2003.

77. "U. N. chief killed in Baghdad explosion," August 19, 2003, *CNN.com,*
http://www.cnn.com/2003/WORLD/meast/08/19/sprj.irq.main/index.html Accessed August 19, 2003.

78. Nazila Fathi, "Iran confirms test of missiles that is able to hit Israel," *New York Times,* July 8, 2003, Page 8, Column 1.

79. Steven R. Weisman, "U.S. to Send Signal to North Koreans in Naval Exercise," *New York Times,* August 18, 2003.

80. Neil MacFarquhar, "Rising Tide of Islamic Militants see Iraq as Ultimate Battlefield," *New York Times,* August 13, 2003.

SECTION TWO

ELECTIONS, REFORMS, AND THE BUSH PRESIDENCY

Presidential Election 2000

The 2000 presidential election between Republican candidate George W. Bush, and Democratic candidate Vice President Al Gore proved to be a dead-heat contest that came down to counting and recounting the last few votes in the election-determining state of Florida. The outcome of the election took 5 weeks to determine as recounts in certain counties raised serious question about how votes were being interpreted if the chad punched from the ballot card was not completely remove (thus producing a 'hanging chad' controversy) or if 'dimples' were left on the ballot that caused ballot counters to question the intent of the voter. As the investigation into the election process progressed, it became clear that there was no uniformity of interpretation of voter intent across counties in Florida, and that the problem was not limited to Florida. Many states lacked statewide rules for interpreting voter intent when the mark on the ballot was not clear. For instance, most of the 32 states using punch cards for ballots required that two corners of the chad be detached in order to be counted as a vote, while in Texas and Washington state, dimpled chads could be counted as a vote. On Dec. 12, 2000, the U.S Supreme Court called a halt to the vote recount in Florida based on the fact that voter intent was being interpreted differently from county to county in Florida, and concluded that "the vast majority of states appear to have recount laws that would likely be found unconstitutional under *Bush v. Gore.*" The court concluded that voters' constitutional rights to equal protection under the law were being violated. The 5-4 Supreme Court decision gave the Florida election to Bush with a 537 vote margin.[1] This allowed Bush to win the electoral votes in Florida, and thus the electoral college election nationally, even though Gore had won the popular vote by 540,000.[2]

The intense controversy over the 2000 presidential election outraged voters, and awakened Americans to the reality that one of their basic rights, to vote and have that vote count, had been called into serious question. The votes of tens of thousands of voters in Florida were not counted because of errors in the vote counting procedures or because their names had been wrongly removed from the voter registrations list.[3]

A *New York Times* investigation into the election process in Florida revealed that in the days following the election, there was a Republican drive to persuade canvassing boards in the Bush strongholds to waive Florida's election laws when counting overseas absentee ballots and to disqualify oversees ballots in counties won by Vice President Al Gore, and concluded that these 'adjustments' in local election law, played a key role in the election outcomes. An analysis of 2,490 ballots counted as legal votes after Election Day found 680 questionable votes, with 80 percent of them accepted in counties Bush carried. Overseas ballots were judged by markedly different standards, depending on where they were counted. In interviews with voters, some admitted to casting illegal ballots after Election Day. There was no evidence that either political party organized efforts to solicit late votes.[4]

The most disturbing finding in the 2000 election was reported by the U. S. Commission on Civil Rights. According to their in-depth investigation of poll data, spoiled ballots, and testimonies of 100 citizens and state officials, some of the problems in Florida appeared to have been racially motivated. Black voters were nearly 10 times more likely than non-black voters to have their ballots rejected. The Commission estimated that 14.4 percent of the black votes in Florida were rejected, compared to 1.6 percent of the non-black vote.[5] The Commission concluded that salient feature of the 2000 election was NOT the closeness of the contest, but the disenfranchisement of Florida voters. The Commission defined disenfranchised voters as "individuals who are entitled to vote, want to vote, or attempt to vote, but who are deprived from either voting or having their votes counted."[6] The investigation did not find that the highest officials of the state conspired to disenfranchise voters. It did, however, conclude that the state's highest officials, who were responsible for "ensuring efficiency, uniformity, and fairness in the election" had failed to meet their charge.[7]

A report from the General Accounting Office (GAO) reported that 57% of the precincts across the country experienced difficulties with voter eligibility, accessibility of polling places, technology, and poorly

27

trained poll workers. The GAO and civic interest groups recommended election reforms in the areas of:

- Voter registration;
- Absentee and early voting;
- Election day administration; and
- Vote counts, certification, and recounts.[8]

Election Reform

The disputes over the 2000 presidential election and subsequent studies over the problems revealed serious flaws in the election system ranging from antiquated equipment to questionable registration and voting procedures. Following the election, the public pressured state and federal officials to take seriously the problems with the voting system. In the year following the election, more than 1800 pieces of legislation were introduced to state legislatures, and 250 new laws were enacted. Nearly 50 bills were introduced into the house and senate.[9]

In October, 2002, the Senate passed election reform bill H.R. 3295. The bill provides $3.86 billion over 4 years to upgrade voting equipment and to improve voting and voter registration procedures, as well as funds for training for poll workers. Specific mandates of the bill include:

- By Jan. 1, 2004 new registering voters must provide a driver's license number or the last eight digits of their social security number. For voters without either of these, state officials will assign a number;
- By the 2004 presidential election, states are required to provide provisional ballots to voters whose names do not appear on the registration list. When the voter's eligibility is verified, the vote will be counted;
- By 2006, all states must have a statewide computerized voter registration database;
- By 2006 all voting equipment must provide for 'second chance' voting, which will allow voters to correct errors on their ballots before casting them.

- All polling places must have at least one voting station accessible by handicapped persons.

Some civil rights groups opposed the identification provision of the bill fearing it would have a disproportionate impact on Hispanics, and discourage Latino voters.[10]

The George W. Bush Presidency

George W. Bush became the 43rd president of the United States after losing the popular vote to Al Gore and narrowly winning the Electoral College majority in a vote count dispute in Florida.[11] Dubbed the 'accidental president' after such a narrow victory, the President was quick to win the public's trust and confidence in his ability to run the nation. His approval ratings have consistently stayed high, between 50% and 60%. His highest rating of 90% occurred in response to his handling of 9/11 (see figure 2.1)[12]

Figure 2.1

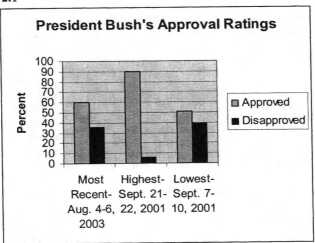

Source: The Gallup Organization; State of the Nation;
http://www.gallup.com/poll/stateNation/

During his campaign, President Bush promised to cut taxes, reform schools, build the defense, and to approach social welfare concerns with "compassionate conservatism," favoring funding faith-based groups for addressing welfare needs.[13] While his domestic agenda has taken second priority to the war on terrorism, President Bush has remained true to his campaign promises in pursuing his domestic agenda, having achieved tax cuts and school reform during his first year in office, and promising more legislation and funding to address social concerns at home in the last two years of his term.[14]

President Bush's values and ideology that has guided his election campaign and presidency reflects that of his conservative party, especially in regard to unregulated the market forces and supporting the expansion of business in the private sector. Favoring a mix of consumer side and supply side economics, President Bush has successfully passed a series of tax cuts totally $1.7 trillion, in an effort to stimulate the sluggish economy by increasing consumer spending, and encouraging business investment and the creation of new jobs.[15] Some financial analyst have concerns over the size of the tax cut claiming it was too large to be fiscally responsible, and skewed to give greater benefits to those with higher income levels.[16] Indeed, President Bush has received his lowest marks in his handling of the economy (see figure 2.2) with a 25% 'excellent' rating and 75% 'fair/poor' rating. This tends to overshadow the publics general satisfaction with the state of the country (46% v. 52% dissatisfied) (see figure 2.2).[17]

Also in line with conservative party values, is the President's stance on abortion. On his first day in office, he rallied supported of anti-abortion groups when he reinstated a policy prohibiting any federal funding of family-planning groups that offer abortion services or abortion counseling overseas. This policy was first instated by President Ronald Reagan, and rescinded by President Clinton in 1993.[18]

A big success during his first year in office was President Bush's passage of The No Child Left Behind Act of 2001. It provides some of the most sweeping school reforms since 1965, and redefines the federal role in K-12 education by targeting the achievement gap between disadvantaged and minority students and their peers.[19] The law requires states to put implement a set of standards, and comprehensive testing to assure that standards are met.. The act is intended to provide common standards and accountability to those standards across schools nationally.[20]

Figure 2.2

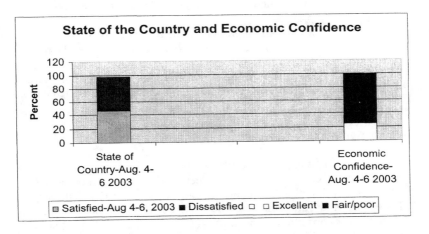

Source: The Gallup Organization; State of the Nation;
http://www.gallup.com/poll/stateNation/

President Bush's domestic agenda for 2003-2004 promises to address the wide range of social welfare needs at home and abroad. These are summarized below:

- Passage of a faith-based initiative to address the needs of poor, homeless, and addicted Americans;
- $400 million in Medicare reform;
- Repairs to the Social Security retirement system;
- Passage of the Citizen Service Act [HR 4854], that proposes to amends the National and Community Service Act of 1990 (NCSA) and the Domestic Volunteer Service Act of 1973 (DVSA), and reauthorize for 5 years the programs administered by the

Corporation for National and Community Service ("The Corporation"). These programs are: Senior Corps, AmeriCorps, and Lean & Serve America;[21]

- $450 million initiative that would bring mentors to disadvantaged junior high students and children of prisoners.
- $600-million program to help an additional 300,000 Americans receive drug abuse treatment over the next three years; and,
- Emergency Plan for AIDS Relief – a $15 billion to treat and prevent AIDS infections in the most afflicted nations of Africa and the Caribbean.[22]

Campaign Finance Reform

The rules of campaign contribution began being formed in the early part of the 20th century, when it was deemed illegal for corporations to spend money directly on election campaigns under the 1907 Tillman Act. It was feared that allowing corporations to donate to political campaigns would foster corruption of the political process. The first federal laws requiring campaign finance disclosure were passed in 1910 and 19/11. Then in 1947, labor unions were banned from spending money on federal elections under the Taft-Hartley Act. To further safeguard the election process, in 1974 limits were set on the amount of money individuals could contribute to individual federal candidates ($1000) or to a political party ($20,000/yr.) for the purpose of influencing a federal election.[23]

Soft money is any money received by candidates or political parties that violate these rules. During the 1988 presidential campaign, these rules were circumvented by democratic candidate Michael Dukakis and republican candidate George H. W. Bush. Both candidates campaigned aggressively for soft money saying that it was being used for 'party building' activities, and not being spend directly on the election. Since then, soft money contributions have continued to grow allowing big business and powerful unions to have ready access to and undue influence over the politicians they contribute to. The amount of soft money raised by political candidates and parties has grown drastically from $86 million in 1992 to $470 million in the 2001-2002 election cycle.[24] Figure 2.3 depicts the trends in the use of soft money since

1992. It is readily acknowledged among political parties and candidates that soft money is routinely used to influence elections. [25]

Figure 2.3

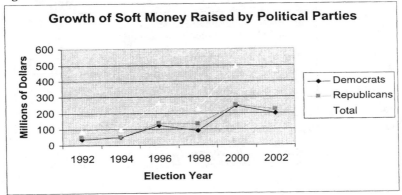

Data Source: CQ Researcher, Nov. 22, 2002, Vol. 12, No. 41, p. 972;
and Common Cause,
    Campaign Finance Reform, Report: The Soft Money Finale!
    http://www.commoncause.org/news/default.cfm?ArtID=129
    Accessed August 20, 2003.

The amount of soft money that political parties raised tended to dramatically escalate on presidential election years (1996 & 2000) and moderate or retract on congressional only election years (for instance, 1998 & 2002).

When corporation and other special interest groups contribute large sums of money, usually something is expected in return. Numerous examples have surfaced over the years that suggested that big political spenders have won themselves big corporate welfare benefits in exchange for political contributions.[26] Table 2.1 list the top ten donors for all soft money, and tables 2.2 & 2.3 list the top donors by party[27] during the 2001-2002 election cycle. These are the companies and individuals who have ready access to and influence over elected officials.

Table 2.1: Top Ten Soft Money Donor Categories
January 1, 2001 to November 5, 2002 *(In $ Millions)*

Donor Category	Amount Donated
1. Securities and Investments	$34.4
2. Telecommunications	29.1
3. Entertainment & Media	27.7
4. Pharmaceuticals and Medical Supplies	22.7
5. Computer and Electronics	19.7
6. Real Estate	19.0
7. Insurance	18.6
8. Trial Lawyers	17.4
9. Banks & Lenders	15.8
10. Oil & Gas	9.9

Information collected from 'Common Cause' website:
http://www.commoncause.org/news/default.cfm?ArtID=129

Table 2.2: Top Ten Soft Money Donors to Republican National
Party Committee
January 1, 2001-November 5, 2002 *(In $ Millions)*

Donor	Amount Donated
1. American Financial Group	$3.4
2. Pharmaceutical Research & Manufacturers of America	3.3
3. Texans for John Cornyn	3.1
4. Philip Morris Cos Inc	2.3
5. Presidential Inaugural Committee	2.1
6. Microsoft Corp	1.9
7. AT&T	1.8
8. Governor Bush Committee	1.7
9. Freddie Mac	1.6
10. Fulton, Stanley E., *Founder, Anchor Gaming*	1.3

Information collected from 'Common Cause' website:
http://www.commoncause.org/news/default.cfm?ArtID=129

To counter this growing and ominous trend of soft money usage, Senators John McCain (R-AZ) and Russell Feingold (D-WI) sponsored the Bipartisan Campaign Reform Act (BCRA) of 2002, also known as McCain-Feingold bill. The law aims at preventing special interests dollars from pouring into federal election campaigns by banning national parties from raising soft money. The law also seeks to close issue-advertising loophole by barring groups from airing TV advertisements close to elections.[28] BCRA went into effect Nov. 6, 2002, the day after the mid-term elections, but has been challenged on its constitutionality in the U.S. District Court for the District of Columbia. Opponents say that it infringes on their First Amendment right of free speech. The Court issued a fragmented decision stating that at least four components of the law were unconstitutional. The decision was appealed at the U.S. Supreme Court who will hear the case in the fall/winter of 2003/2004. Until that time, the Supreme Court has ordered that the law remain in effect in its entirety, thus nullifying the U.S. District Court's ruling.[29] The Supreme Court's [at least temporary] overruling of the lower court's decision is significant in a presidential election cycle since it dramatically limits the amount of money that candidates can raise compared to previous years. Candidates will be forced to rely solely on 'hard money.'

Table 2.3: Top Ten Soft Money Donors to
Democratic National Party Committee
January 1, 2001-November 5, 2002
(In $ Millions)

Donor	*Amount Donated*
1. Saban, Haim, *Chair, Saban Entertainment*	$9.3
2. American Federation of State, County, and Municipal Employees	7.5
3. Eychaner, Fred, *President, Newsweb Co.; Owner, WPWR*	7.4
4. Bing, Stephen L.,	7.1

	Producer, Shangra-La Entertainment	
5.	Service Employees International Union (SEIU)	4.9
6.	Communication Workers of America	4.0
7.	United Brotherhood of Carpenters & Joiners	3.9
8.	American Federation of Teachers	3.4
9.	Kirsch, Steven, *CEO, Propel*	3.3
10.	Laborers' International Union of North America	2.3

Information collected from 'Common Cause' website:
http://www.commoncause.org/news/default.cfm?ArtID=129

Hard money is contributions by individuals and Political Action Committees (PAC) that fall within the contribution limits of the law, and can be used directly in the election of federal candidates. The new BCRA increased the amount of hard money that candidates can raise for election purposes, and was effective January 1, 2003. Individual contributions were doubled to $2000 per candidate per election and were indexed for inflation. The individual aggregate amounts were increased to $95,000 ($37,500 to candidates and $57,500 to political parties and PACs). PAC contribution limits remain at $5000 per candidate per election, plus $15,000 to a national party committee and $5,000 combined to state and local party committees.[30]

President Bush's ability to raise campaign funds has been well above what his opponents have been able to muster. Currently, his re-election fund drive for election 2004 is at $42 million and aiming for $200 million.[31] This compares to a range of $3.1 to $12.9 million raised by Democratic contenders (see table 2.4).[32]

Table 2.4: Hard Money Raised by
Democratic Presidential Candidates
(As of June 30, 2003)

Candidate	Amount Raised (In Millions)
Senator John Kerry (D-MA)	$12.9
Senator John Edwards (D- NC)	11.9
Howard Dean (D-Former Governor of VT)	10.2
Rep. Richard Gephardt (D-)MO	9.8
Senator Joseph Lieberman (D-CT)	8.2
Senator Bob Graham (D-FL)	3.1

Source: PoliticalMoneyline, http://www.tray.com/cgi-win/indexhtml.exe?MBF=pres

ENDNOTES

1. Kathy Koch "Election Reform" *The CQ Researcher,* November 02, 2001 Vol. 11, No. 38.
2. Kenneth Jost, "The Bush Presidency," *The CQ Researcher,* February 2, 2001, Vol. 11, No. 4.
3. Thomas Mann, "An Agenda for Election Reform" June, 2001, *Brookings Institution Policy Brief No. 82,* June 2001.
4. David Barstow and Don Van Natta Jr., "EXAMINING THE VOTE; How Bush Took Florida: Mining the Overseas Absentee Vote," July 15, 2001, *New York Times,* Section 1, Page 1 , Column 1.
5. U.S. Commission on Civil Rights, *Voting Irregularities in Florida During the 2000 Presidential Election,* Executive Summary June 8, 2001, Washington DC pp. 1-7 http://www.usccr.gov/ Accessed August 23, 2003.
6. Ibid p.2
7. Ibid p.2
8. U.S. General Accounting Office, Elections: Perspectives on Activities and Challenges Across the Nation GAO-02-3, October 15, 2001, Washington DC.
9. Kathy Koch "Election Reform" *The CQ Researcher,* November 02, 2001 Vol. 11, No. 38.
10. Edward Walsh, "Election Reform Bill is Passed by Senate," *Washington Post,* October 17, 2002.

11. Kenneth Jost, "The Bush Presidency," *The CQ Researcher*, February 2, 2001, Vol. 11, No. 4.

12. The Gallup Organization, *State of the Nation,* http://www.gallup.com/poll/stateNation/ , Accessed August 23, 2003.

13. Kenneth Jost, "The Bush Presidency," *The CQ Researcher*, February 2, 2001, Vol. 11, No. 4.

14. President George W. Bush, *State of the Union Address*, January 28, 2003, Washington DC. http://www.whitehouse.gov/news/releases/2003/01/20030128-19.html Accessed August 23, 2003.

15. William M. Welch and Laurence McQuillan, "Deficit outlook soars to $455B," USA TODAY, July 15, 2003, http://www.usatoday.com/news/washington/2003-07-15-record-deficit_x.htm Accessed August 23. 2003.

16. Kenneth Jost, "The Bush Presidency," *The CQ Researcher*, February 2, 2001, Vol. 11, No. 4.

17. The Gallup Organization, *State of the Nation,* http://www.gallup.com/poll/stateNation/ Accessed August 23, 2003.

18. Kenneth Jost, "The Bush Presidency," *The CQ Researcher*, February 2, 2001, Vol. 11, No. 4.

19. U.S. Department of Education, *No Child Left Behind Act of 2001,* Washington DC http://www.ed.gov/offices/OESE/esea/ Accessed August 23, 2003.

20. Paul E. Peterson and Martin R. West, eds., *No Child Left Behind? The politics and practice of school accountability* 2003, (Washington DC: The Brookings Institution Press).

21. Corporation for National and Community Service, http://www.nationalservice.org/whatshot/pendinglegislation.html Accessed August 23, 2003.

22. President George W. Bush, *State of the Union Address*, January 28, 2003, Washington DC. http://www.whitehouse.gov/news/releases/2003/01/20030128-19.html Accessed August 23, 2003.

23. Kenneth Jost, "Campaign Finance Showdown," *CQ Researcher*, November 22, 2002, Vol. 12. No. 41 pp. 969-992.

24. "Soft Money: What is it and why is it a problem?" *Common Cause, 2000,*

http://www.commoncause.org/laundromat/stat/softmoney.cfm
Accessed August 20, 2003.

25. Kenneth Jost, "Campaign Finance Showdown," *CQ Researcher*, November 22, 2002, Vol. 12. No. 41 pp. 969-992.

26. "The Enormous growth of soft money," *Common Cause,* 2000, http://www.commoncause.org/laundromat/stat/growing.cfm Accessed August 20, 2003. For case information regarding paybacks see "Going for broke: Big money, big banks & bankruptcy" *Common Cause,* 1998, http://www.commoncause.org/publications/goingforbroke.htm "Drilling for bargains," *Common Cause,* 1998, http://www.commoncause.org/publications/drilling.htm, and other cases at the Common Cause web site, Accessed August 20, 2003.

27. "Report: The soft money finale! *Common Cause,* April &, 2003, http://www.commoncause.org/news/default.cfm?ArtID=129Acc essed August 20, 2003.

28. Kenneth Jost, "Campaign Finance Showdown," *CQ Researcher*, November 22, 2002, Vol. 12. No. 41 pp. 969-992.

29. "Three-judge panel blocks its own campaign finance ruling, Supreme Court will decide McCain-Feingold's fate," Center for Individual Freedom, May 22, 2003, http://www.cfif.org/htdocs/legal_issues/legal_updates/first_amen dment_cases/mccain_feingold_fate.htm Accessed August 20, 2003.

30. Kenneth Jost, "Campaign Finance Showdown," *CQ Researcher,* November 22, 2002, Vol. 12, No. 41 p. 974.

31. "Political Money Put to the Test," *New York Times.com*, August 19, 2003, http://www.nytimes.com/2003/08/19/19UE2.htme?th Accessed August 20, 2003.

32. "Guide to presidential races," *PoliticalMoneyline,* June 30, 2003, http://www.tray.com/cgi-win/indexhtml.exe?MBF=pres Accessed August 20, 2003.

SECTION THREE

THE ECONOMIC STATE OF THE NATION

The Boon and Bust Economy

The decade of the 1990's saw an unprecedented economic boon as the stock market expanded at astronomical rates. The optimism of investors in the new technology market caused stocks to soar and profits to amass. Profits supported new business investments that added more fuel to the growing economy. The invention of the World Wide Web facilitated the commercialization of the internet and the expansion of dot.com companies. There were other factors during the second half of the 1990's that boosted the economy and public confidence as well. The fall of the Berlin wall in 1989 and the end of the Cold war provided economic opportunities in regions of the world that, until these events occurred, had been inaccessible to business investors. The end of the Cold War also meant a decline in defense outlays. These events, combined with increases in individual and corporate earnings and thus, increases in federal tax receipts, helped swing the federal budget from a deficit to a surplus by the end of the decade. Another piece of the economic success story of the 1990's was the election of a conservative congress in 1994, and a president committed to downsizing government.[1] In his 1996 State of the Union address, President Clinton informed the nation that "The era of big government is over."[2]

The rapid growth of the stock market during the 1990's produced what has become know as the 'stock market bubble.' Such 'bubbles' occur when favorable events, such as those discussed above, occur suddenly and unexpectedly, producing unrealistic optimism about the future performance of the stock market, and unsustainable performance levels, causing an "irrational exuberance" about the market. An example of how the market behaves under the influence of "irrational exuberance" is the public response to the offering of Netscape stock. In spite of the fact that Netscape had lost $4.3 million of revenues in the first 6 months of 1995, when its stock hit the market, the trading in the first day resulted in a market capitalization of $2.2 billion. Under such economic frenzy, businesses tend to over invest in capital assets (believing that these

40

economic conditions will continue indefinitely) and/or malinvest, that is, buy the wrong capital assets to produce the goods and services to meet demand. (For instance, a movie company invests in equipment to make VHS videos, when the market demand is for DVDs).[3]

When a 'bubble' is created such as that during the mid and late 1990's, it makes the economy vulnerable to uncertainty. Since economies around the world have grown more interdependent over the past 15 years, when economic crisis occurs in one region of the world, it has an impact in other regions. Two events in the late 1990's had negative impacts on the U.S. economy that eventually gave way to the bursting of the stock market bubble. First, was the Asian financial crisis in 1997[4] followed by the Russian default on all foreign loans in 1998.[5] These global economic events shook investor confidence regarding the global market. A direct impact was felt in the telecommunication and information technology markets. The technology market went from an after-tax profit of $21.6 billion in 1996 to an after-tax loss of $27.9 billion in 2000. From January 2000 to January 2001, the NASDAQ stock market dropped by 45%. The stock market bubble had burst.[6]

With profits gone, businesses began to contract, business investments sharply declined and companies began to close. Since December, 2000, 60% of all corporate defaults have been in the telecommunication sectors. Jobs in the technology market fell away dramatically. By March 2001, the country was in a recession which extended to November, 2001. While economic growth in the Gross Domestic Product (GDP) rose to 2.7% in the fourth quarter of 2001 (from -1.6% in the second quarter of 2001), the economy remained sluggish.[7] The unemployment rate peaked in June, 2003 to 6.4% and then began to decline in July to 6.2%. Workers claiming unemployment benefits ranged from 3.3-3.7 million from 2001-2003.[8]

Other unexpected events continued to batter the economy in the months following the burst of the stock market bubble. The terrorists' attacks on New York and Washington shattered the public's confidence in not only our economy, but our very way of life. Massive numbers of lives, businesses, and property were lost with the collapse of the World Trade Center. In the months and years that followed, New York suffered a much more severe recession than the rest of the nation. Through March

2001-March 2003, New York suffered a 3.2% loss of jobs compared to 1.9% loss for the nation as a whole.[9] The 'war on terror' that followed 9/11 escalated federal defense and homeland security spending turning the federal budget from a surplus to a deficit.

In October, 2001, Enron Corporation unexpectedly announced a big quarterly loss and a huge write-down in shareholder equity. In the months that followed, corporate scandal swept through Enron and Arthur Anderson, their accounting firm, and executives were charged with fraud and creating off-book partnerships. Close on the heals of the Enron scandal were other large corporations caught up in fraud, insider trading, and grand larceny (Adelphia Communications, ImClone Systems, Tyco International, and WorldCom Inc. to name a few). The illegal accounting practices, earning shortfalls, bankruptcies, and criminal indictments over the next year severely shook investor confidence in the stock market.[10] In a telephone poll to 1,003 adult Americans in July, 2002, 72% said that they did not believe that the accounting scandals being revealed in the news were isolated incidences, but indicated a pattern of deception among large corporations. Seventy-one percent believed that the typical CEO was less honest and ethical than the average person, and overall, Americans had less trust in CEOs, major corporations, stockbrokers and the stock market after the scandals (see figures 3.1-3.2 & table 3.1)[11]

Figure 3.1

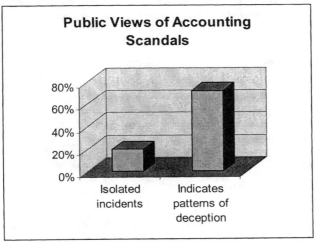

Source: From Time/CNN telephone poll of 1,003 adult Americans,

July 10-11, 2002

Figure 3.2

Source: From Time/CNN telephone poll of 1,003 adult Americans,
July 10-11, 2002

Boosting the Sluggish Economy

Economic policymakers implemented two types of policies in response to the national recession and resistant economy from 2001-2003. First, The Federal Reserve progressively lowered interest rates that pushed lending interest rates low. This boosted consumer spending especially in the areas of homes and automobiles. The second type of policies implemented were a series of tax relief measures put forth by President Bush and enacted by the Congress. The purpose of the tax relief packages was two fold. First, tax relief aimed to return money to the pockets of Americans to stimulate consumption and thus put a demand on production. Second, tax relief to businesses hoped to stimulate business investments and the creation of jobs. This is a combination consumer side and supply side economic practices, or a mixed economic approach.[12] The three tax relief bills that were enacted from 2001-2003 were:

- The Economic Growth and Tax Relief Reconciliation Act of 2001 (Enacted June 2001);
- The Job Creation and Worker Assistance Act of 2002 (Enacted March 2002); and,
- The Jobs and Growth Tax Relief Reconciliation Act of 2003 (Enacted May, 2003)[13]

Table 3.1: Americans Have Less Trust in Business

Yes, I have less trust in...	%
CEOs of major U.S. corporations	69
Major U.S. corporations	59
The Stock Market	53
Stockbrokers	50

Source: From Time/CNN telephone poll of 1,003 adult Americans, July 10-11, 2002

The first tax bill, The Economic Growth and Tax Relief Reconciliation Act of 2001, cut taxes and returned dollars to American households to help stimulate consumer buying. It also increased the child tax credit to $1000. Many of the provisions in this bill were accelerated by the 2003 tax relief bill. The second tax relief bill focused on providing businesses with tax relief in order to boost business investments. Additional tax credits and bonuses were made available to businesses in the New York City 'Liberty Zone,' those areas most impacted by 9/11. The Job Creation and Worker Assistance Act of 2002 extended unemployment benefits of unemployed workers and extended tax credits that expired in 2001 to employers who hired workers belonging to underprivileged groups and recipients participating in welfare to work programs.[14] One year after the passage of The Job Creation and Worker Assistance Act the economy was starting to respond, but slowly. The economic growth rate crept to around 3 percent.[15]

President Bush's third round of tax cuts was signed into law on May 28, 2003 as the Jobs and Growth Tax Relief Reconciliation Act of 2003 (JGTR). Aiming to increase consumer buying through tax cuts and grow jobs with business incentives, JGTR accelerated many of the provisions included in the Economic Growth and Tax Relief

45

Reconciliation Act of 2001. The law was effective January 1, 2003, and provides temporary tax relief through 2008.[16] Primary features of the bill included:

- Increases the child tax credit from $600 to $1000 for 2003 and 2004. In 2005 it will fall back to $700 and will gradually rise to $1000 by 2010;
- Increases the standard deduction for married filers to double that of single filers for 2003 and 2004. In 2005 the standard deduction for married filers will fall to 174% of single filers and gradually increase to 200% by 2009;
- Reduces tax rates to 10% for lowest income earners and 35% for highest income earners (15, 25, 28, 33% for intervening tax brackets) for 2003 and 2004;
- Reduces capital gains taxes for 2003-2009;
- Provides business incentives through expanded expensing thresholds and bonus depreciation; and
- Extends tax payments for corporate taxpayers from September 15, 2003 to October 1, 2003. [17]

JGTR also appropriated $20 billion to be distributed among the 50 states as a tax relief measure.[18]

States Struggle to Balance Budgets

Like the federal government, state budgets suffered under the declining economy. Unlike the federal government, all states, except for Vermont, are required to balance the state budget every year. States also experienced a second fiscal insult from the tax cuts passed by Congress in 2001, 2002, and 2003. Some state taxes are tied to federal tax rates, so as federal rates decline, so do state income tax rates. Other fiscal hardships for states included the rising cost of Medicaid, a program with federal and state shared funding, and federal spending mandates to states in homeland security, education, and election reform. Almost every state experienced budget crisis from 2001-2003.[19]

States who faced budget overruns used a number of tactics to stave off budget deficits and to balance their budgets. Some were forced to cut programs and/or raise taxes. Others raised tuition and cut enrollments at state-run colleges. Health care services were cut and one state released 567 low-level felons from prison to save money. Some states put a freeze on hiring and wages, and did not replaced workers who retired or resigned. Fifteen states laid off employees, and 13 reorganized programs to cut spending.[20] States cut between $20-40 billion from their spending from 2001-2003, with more expected in the 2004 fiscal cycle beginning July 1, 2003. Some contend that the cuts in state spending have had a disproportionate impact on the poor.[21]

With the passage of the Job and Growth Tax Relief Reconciliation Act of 2003 in May, 2003, states received an important boost in their economies. Congress appropriate $20 billion to be distributed among states based on population. States were required to earmark half of their relief dollars for Medicaid, the state and federally funded health care program that serves 47 million low-income and disabled citizens. States were free to use the other half of their relief package as they deemed best.[22]

From Federal Surplus to Federal Deficit

The booming economy of the 1990's did much to reduce the federal deficit from a peak of $290 billion in 1992 to a surplus of $236 billion in 2000.[23] Economic expansion during this period boosted tax receipts and lowered interest rates which in turn reduced government's interest expenses. Medicare and Medicaid spending was restrained during this period as well by a slower than normal growth in medical costs. A major factor contributing to the shrinking deficit was fiscal policy changes made by the 1990 and 1993 deficit-reduction law, The Budget Enforcement Act (BEA), tightened Medicare reimbursements to providers and increased income and excise taxes. For fiscal years 1991-1995, the BEA imposed 2 budget restrictions: 1) it capped nominal discretionary spending at $550 billion during this period, which effectively limited defense and non-defense discretionary spending, and 2) tied entitlement spending (such as social security) to tax increases and/or decreases. Tax reduction was prohibited without also reducing entitlement spending. Likewise, any increase in entitlement spending required an increase in taxes as well.[24]

The unexpected war effort and growth in military spending secondary to the 9/11 and the subsequent 'war on terrorism,' the creation and funding of the Department of Homeland Security, tax cuts, and sluggish economy are the major factors that account for the growing federal deficit (see figure 3.3).[25]

Figure 3.3

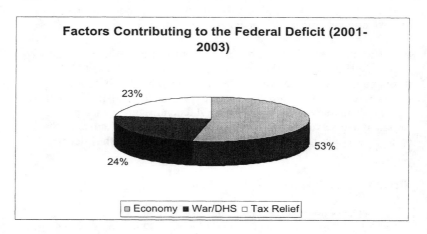

Source: Office of Management and Budget,
http://www.whitehouse.gov/omb/charts/msr-charts.html

Growth in federal spending on defense, homeland security, and non-defense spending from 2001-2004 accounted for some of the growing deficit. For instance, defense spending increased by 5% in 2001, 8% in 2002, 11% in 2003, and is estimated to decline in the 2004 budget by 4% (see table 3.2 & figure 3.4). This, of course, does not take into account unexpected developments on the war on terrorism, peacekeeping and reconstruction in Iraq, and other developments that may occur in Afghanistan. The greatest increase in spending occurred in the newly created Department of Homeland Security (DHS), with a growth increase from 14% in 2001 to 86% in 2003 when it was legitimized by congress. DHS growth rate is estimated to be down in 2004 to 20%. By comparison, the growth of non-defense spending has declined every year since 2001 (15%), and is estimated to have a growth rate of only 2% in 2004.[26]

Table 3.2: Growth in Federal Spending 2001-2004
(Percent of Change)

	Defense %	Homeland Security %	Non-Defense %
2001	5	14	15
2002	8	21	6
2003	11	86	5
2004 (est.)	**4**	**20**	**2**

Source: Office of Management and Budget,
http://www.whitehouse.gov/omb/charts/msr-charts.html

Figure 3.4

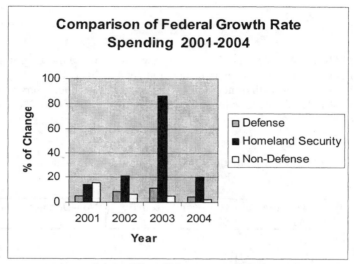

Source: Office of Management and Budget,
http://www.whitehouse.gov/omb/charts/msr-charts.html

Federal revenues declined two years in a row and in 2002 revenues were lowered by 7 percent, the largest decline since 1946. The burst of the stock market bubble was followed by a disappearance of tens of billions of highly taxed income. For instance, in 2000, the top five percent of the population paid 56 percent of individual income taxes. This was the income bracket that was most hit by the dramatic stock market decline in 2001, which resulted in the rapid plummet in tax receipts in 2001 and 2002. The office of Management and Budget (OMB) projected in the 2004 federal budget that the deficit will continue to grow through 2004, and expects the deficit growth to begin to recede in 2005 (see figure 3.5).[27]

Figure 3.5

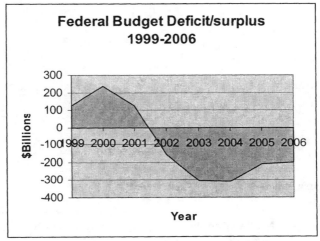

Source: Office of Management and Budget

The Impact of the Economy on People's Lives

The median household income declined by 2.2% overall from 2000-2001 from $43,162 to $42,228.[28] Married couple families' income remained stable with only a slight decline that was not statistically significant. Female headed families without a husband present saw a 3.1% decline in income from $29,053 to $28,142. Male headed families without a wife present experienced the greatest family income decline of 6% from $43,332 to $40,715 (see figure 3.6).[29]

Women working full-time year round faired the best by increasing their incomes from 2000-2001 from $28,228 to $29,215, while the income of men working full-time year round remained the same. This raised the female-to-male earning ration from .74 to .76. These income estimates were based solely on earned income before taxes, and did not include the value of employment fringe benefits, or government subsidies such as cash or in-kind assistance (see figure 3.7).[30]

Figure 3.6

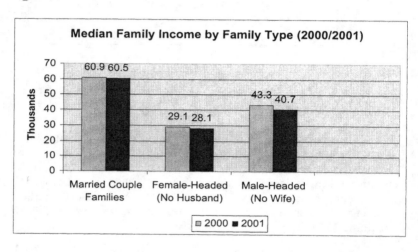

Source: U.S. Census Bureau, Money Income in the United States: 2001

Figure 3.7

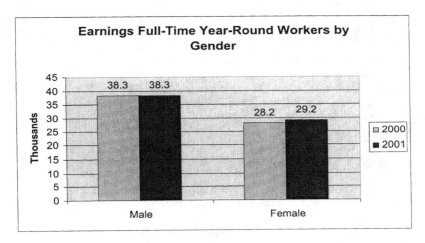

Source: U.S. Census Bureau, Money Income in the United States: 2001

When the impact of the declining economy is examined by race, Asians/Pacific Islanders, and Blacks were hit the hardest. Blacks experienced a 3.4% decline in income while Asians/Pacific Islanders lost 6.4% of their income. Whites and Hispanics showed the slowest decline in incomes (1.4% and 1.6% respectively) (see table 3.3).[31]

Table 3.3: Change in Median Income by Race
2000-2001

	2000	**2001**	% of Change
All Races	$43,162	$42,228	**-2.2**
White	45,142	44,517	**-1.4**
Black	30,495	29,470	**-3.4**
Hispanic	34,094	33,565	**-1.6**
Asian & Pacific Islander	**57,313**	**53,635**	**-6.4**

Source: U.S. Census Bureau, Money Income in the United States: 2001

The disparity of wealth between the 'haves' and 'have nots' continued to increase through 2001. For instance, the lower economic class (lowest 20% by earnings) captured 3.9 percent of all earnings in the county in 1990. By 2001, it had declined to 3.5% with a .1% decline from 2000-2001 (see table 3.4). Likewise, the lower middle class (second lowest 20% of earnings) represented 9.6% of all earnings in 1990 but only 8.7 % in 2001, representing a decline of .9% with .2% occurring from 200-2001. In fact, four of the five quintiles (20% divisions) continued to show a decline in earnings from 1990-2001. The exception was the fifth quintile or top 20% of earners, who progressively made gains in earnings from 1990-2001 for a total gain of 3.5%. The top 20% of the population earned 50.1% of all earnings in 2001. An even more dramatic gain occurred for the top 5% of earners who earned 18.6% of all wages in 1990 and 22.4% in 2001, representing a 3.8% increase.[32]

Table 3.4: Income Distribution by Quintile and Top 5%
Selected Years--1990-2001

	1990	1995	2000	2001	Difference from 1990-2001
	%	%	%	%	%
Lower Economic Class (Lowest 20% & 1st Quintile)	3.9	3.7	3.6	3.5	-.4
Lower Middle Economic Class (Second Lowest 20% & 2nd Quintile)	9.6	9.1	8.9.	8.7	-.9
Middle Economic Class (Middle20% & 3rd Quintile)	15.9	15.2	14.8	14.6	-1.3
Upper Middle Economic Class (Second Highest 20% & 4th Quintile)	24	23.3	23	23	-1
Upper Economic Class (Highest 20% & 5th Quintile)	46.6	48.7	49.8	50.1	+3.5
Top 5% of Population	**18.6**	**21**	**22.1**	**22.4**	+3.8

Source: U.S. Census Bureau, Money Income in the United States: 2001

What has the impact of the economic downturn been on people's lives? The U.S. Census Bureau reported an increase in poverty in 2001, the first increase in eight years.[33] Preliminary findings suggest that poverty will continue to rise when the 2002 data are anaylzed.[34] A recent national study indicated that increased demands have been made on social service agencies and charities, many of which went unmet. In a study of 27 cities in 2001 sponsored by the U.S. Conference of Mayors, cities reported that 37% of requests for emergency shelter went unmet— an increase of 13% in one year. For families requesting shelter the rate of service denial was 52%, and 22% increase over the previous year. Most cities also experienced an increase demand for food assistance.[35] Economist estimate that the economic recovery may take several years.

America's Capacity for Giving during Economic Tough Times

American's tend to give in proportion to their economic well-being. When times are good, they give more; when the economy declines, giving contracts. Charitable giving in the US increased by 6 percent from 1999-2000.[33] In contrast, as the economy declined from 2000-2002, so did giving, however not dramatically. In spite of declining wages, Americans continued to give during the economic hard times. Total charitable giving reached an historic level of $240.9 billion in 2002, representing a 1% growth in current dollars and a slight decrease of one half of one percent when adjusted for inflation, compared to 2001 ($238.5 billion). Nonprofit organizations reported an overall gain of .4% in 2002 giving compared to 2001; however, when adjusted for inflation this represented a 1.1% loss in contributions. Giving by individuals increased slightly (.7%) in 2002 when compared to 2001 using current dollars, but when adjusted for inflation, showed a decline of .9% (see table 3.5). Giving by foundations showed a decline in current and adjusted dollars. Increases occurred in corporate giving and in bequest giving (see table 3.5).[34]

Table 3.5: Charitable Giving Comparisons by Type of Contributor
2001 and 2002
(In billions)

Contributors	2002 level	2001 level	% change in current dollars	% change after adjusted for inflation
Individuals	$183.7	$182.5	.7	-.9
Bequests	18.1	17.7	2.0	.4
Foundations	26.9	27.2	-1.2	-2.7
Corporations	**12.2**	**11.0**	**10.5**	**8.8**

Source: Giving USA 2003, The Annual Report on Philanthropy of the year 2002

A national survey of 4000 adults in the spring and summer of 2001 was conducted by Independent Sector, a coalition of leading nonprofits, foundations and corporations found that overall, household giving declined in 2000 by 23-45%, depending on household income. Those with the lowest household incomes showed the lowest decline in giving. Key findings of the study included:

- Households with incomes of $75,000 or more decreased their giving by 33% from $3600 to less than $2500;
- Households with incomes between $50,000 and $75,000 decreased giving by 32% (from $2030 to $1390);
- Households with incomes between $25,000-$50,000 decreased giving by 45% ($1300 to $710; and,
- Households with incomes less than $25,000 decreased giving by 23% ($560 to $430)[35]

The majority of charitable contributions 2002 were made by individuals. Giving by individuals constituted 76.3% of all giving in the U.S., followed by foundations (11.2%), bequests (7.5%) and corporations (5.1%) (see figure 3.8).[36]

Figure 3.8

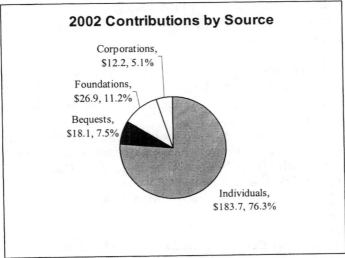

Source: American Association of Fundraising Council, Giving USA 2003.

ENDNOTES

1. United States Congress, Joint Economic Committee, Vice Chairman Jim Saxton (R-NJ), "Economic Repercussions of the Stock Market Bubble: A Joint Economic Committee Study" Washington DC, July, 2003. http://www.house.gov/jec/growth/07-14-03.pdf Accessed August 25, 2003.
2. President Bill Clinton, "State of the Union Address," (Before a Joint Session of the Congress), Washington, DC, January 23, 1996. http://clinton5.nara.gov/WH/New/other/sotu.html Accessed August 26, 2003.
3. United States Congress, Joint Economic Committee, Vice Chairman Jim Saxton (R-NJ), "Economic Repercussions of the Stock Market Bubble: A Joint Economic Committee

Study" Washington DC, July, 2003.
http://www.house.gov/jec/growth/07-14-03.pdf Accessed
August 25, 2003.

4. Ibid

5. "Commentary Russian Default: Four Years Later," *On-line
Pravda*, August 16, 2002.
http://english.pravda.ru/economics/2002/08/16/34706.html
Accessed August 26, 2003.

6. United States Congress, Joint Economic Committee, Vice
Chairman Jim Saxton (R-NJ), "Economic Repercussions of
the Stock Market Bubble: A Joint Economic Committee
Study" Washington DC, July, 2003.
http://www.house.gov/jec/growth/07-14-03.pdf Accessed
August 25, 2003.

7. Ibid.

8. U.S. Labor Department as cited in Sue Kirchoff's "'Job-
loss recovery' sees unemployment claims rise," *USA
TODAY*, July 10, 2003.

9. Public Policy Institute of New York State, "Facts and
Figures about New York's Economy," Albany, New York,
July 25, 2003. http://www.ppinys.org/nyecon.htm
Accessed August 26, 2003.

10. Kenneth Jost, "Corporate Crime," *CQ Researcher,* October
11, 2002, Vol.12, No. 35, pp.1-33.

11. "Public's Trust in CEOs Has Dropped" *Time*/CNN
telephone poll of 1,003 adult Americans, July 10-11, 2002
as cited in Kenneth Jost, "Corporate Crime," *CQ
Researcher,* October 11, 2002, Vol.12, No. 35, p. 10.

12. Kenneth Jost, "Stimulating the Economy," *CQ Researcher,*
January 10, 2003, Vol. 13, No. 1 pp. 1-34.

13. Thomas, Legislative Information on the Internet.
www.thomas.gov Accessed August 25, 2003.

14. Ibid.

15. Budget of the United States Government, Office of
Management and Budget, Washington DC pp.27

http://w3.access.gpo.gov/usbudget/index.html Accessed August 25, 2003.

16. Thomas, Legislative Information on the Internet, http://thomas.loc.gov/cgi-bin/bdquery/z?d108:HR00002:@@@L&summ2=m& Accessed August 25, 2003.

17. Jobs and growth tax relief reconciliation act of 2003 (H.R. 2), "Individual Provisions," National Association of Tax Professionals, Appleton, WI. http://www.natptax.com/taxact2003.pdf Accessed August 25, 2003.

18. Jason White, "Fiscal relief funds fight fires – Real and budgetary" Stateline.org, July 25, 2003, http://www.stateline.org/story.do?storyId=317472 Accessed August 20, 2003.

19. Kenneth Jost, "Stimulating the Economy," *CQ Researcher,* January 10, 2003, Vol. 13 No. 1 31-34.

20. Ibid.

21. Louis Uchitelle, "Red Ink in States Beginning to Hurt Economic Recovery," *New York Times,* July 28, 2003, p. 1, Col. 6.

22. Jason White, "Fiscal relief funds fight fires – Real and budgetary" Stateline.org, July 25, 2003, http://www.stateline.org/story.do?storyId=317472 Accessed August 20, 2003.

23. Budget of the United States Government, Office of management and budget, Historical table 1.1 Summary of Receipts, Outlays, and surpluses or deficits, 1789-2008, Washington DC http://w3.access.gpo.gov/usbudget/fy2004/sheets/hist01z1.xls Accessed August 26, 2003.

24. Alan D. Viard, "The New Budget Outlook: Policymakers Respond to the Surplus," *Economic and Financial Review,* 2nd Quarter, 1999, Federal Reserve Bank of Dallas.

25. Office of Management and Budget, Mid-term charts on fiscal situation, August 26, 20003,

http://www.whitehouse.gov/omb/charts/msr-charts.html
Accessed August 26, 2003.

26. Ibid.

27. Budget of the United States Government, Office of Management and Budget, Washington DC pp.25-26, 311 http://w3.access.gpo.gov/usbudget/index.html Accessed August 25, 2003.

28. Much of the information in this section is taken from the U.S. Census Bureau, "Money income in the United States: 2001," *Current Population Reports: Consumer Income,* Washington DC: Department of Commerce.

29. Ibid., pp. 3-4.

30. Ibid., pp. 2 & 4.

31. Ibid., p. 4.

32. Ibid., p. 19.

33. Bernadette D. Proctor and Joseph Dalaker, *Poverty in the United States: 2001,* U.S. Census Bureau, Current Population Reports, Consumer Income, P60-219 (Washington DC: U.S. Government Printing Office. 2002).

34. American Community Survey Profile Changes 2001-2202. U.S. Census Bureau. http://www.census.gov/acs/www/Products/Profiles/Chg/2002/0102/Tabular/010/01000US3.htm Accessed September 9, 2003.

35. U.S. Conference of Mayors, *A Status Report on Hunger and Homelessness in America's Cities: 2001,* (Washington DC: Author).

36. American Association of Fundraising Counsel, *"Giving USA: The annual report on philanthropy for the year 2001,* (Indianapolis: Author, 2002).

37. American Association of Fundraising Counsel, *"Giving USA: The annual report on philanthropy for the year 2002,* (Indianapolis: Author, 2003).

38. Independent Sector, *Giving in the Tough Times: The impact of personal economic concerns on giving and volunteering.* (Washington DC: Authors, 2001).

39. American Association of Fundraising Counsel, *"Giving USA: The annual report on philanthropy for the year 2002,* (Indianapolis: Author, 2003).

SECTION FOUR

POVERTY, HOMELESSNESS, AND HOUSING IN THE U.S.

Measuring Poverty

Poverty in the United States is determined by a set of income thresholds established by the Census Bureau, and are the official federal measure of poverty in the U. S. Family size, family composition, and age of the head of household are factors used in calculating the income thresholds (see table 4.1).[1] If a family's income falls below the threshold, then they are considered to be living in poverty. The poverty thresholds are updated each year using the Consumer Price Index and reflect changes in inflation; however, cost of living by geographic location is not considered in determining poverty thresholds. Family income is defined as money earned before taxes, but does not include capital gains or non-cash benefits such as housing subsidies or food stamps. Poverty thresholds and the number of people living in poverty are two measures for assessing population well-being, but do not provide a complete description of family need.[2] For instance, the poverty threshold does not tell us the depth of family poverty. For example, two families with four members each report before tax incomes of $10,780 (family 1) and $18,500 (family 2). Both families would be considered officially poor according to the thresholds in table 4.1; however, family 1 is experiencing a much deeper level of poverty than family 2. The depth of poverty is not reflected in the poverty rates determined by the poverty thresholds. All that can be determined is whether a family does or does not meet the poverty threshold.

Table 4.1: Poverty Thresholds by Family Size: 2002

Size of Family Unit	Threshold	Size of Family
Unit Threshold		
One person		Three persons
$14,072		
Under age 65	$ 9,359	Four persons
18,556		
65 and over	8,628	Five persons
22,377		
		Six persons
		25,738
Two persons		Seven persons
29,615		
Householder under 65	12,047	Eight persons
33,121		
Householder 65 and over	10,874	Nine persons of
more 39,843		

Source: US Census Bureau
http://www.census.gov/hhes/poverty/threshld/thresh02.html
Thresholds vary by family composition of the number of adults and children.

The poverty thresholds are primarily used for statistical purposes in calculating poverty rates each year. The poverty thresholds are simplified each year by the Department of Health and Human Services (HHS) and are referred to as *poverty guidelines* (see table 4.2). The poverty guidelines constitute another version of the federal poverty measure, and are issued each year in the *Federal Register*. This simplification is done for administrative purposes. HHS poverty guidelines are used to determine program eligibility for Head Start, the Food Stamp Program, the National School Lunch Program, the Low-Income Home Energy Assistance Program, and the Children's Health Insurance Program. Other public assistance programs such as Temporary Assistance for Needy Families (TANF), Supplemental Security Income (SSI), and the Earned Income Tax Credit (EIC) do not use the poverty guidelines in determining eligibility.[3]

Table 4.2: HHS Poverty Guidelines
(Effective February 7, 2003)

Size of Family Unit	48 Contiguous States and D.C.	Alaska	Hawaii
1	$ 8,980	$11,210	$10,330
2	12,120	15,140	13,940
3	15,260	19,070	17,550
4	18,400	23,000	21,160
5	21,540	26,930	24,770
6	24,680	30,860	28,380
7	27,820	34,790	31,990
8	30,960	38,720	35,600
For each additional person, add	3,140	3,930	3,610

Source: Federal Register, Vol. 68, No. 26, February 7, 2003, pp. 6456-6458.
Note that the Office of Economic Opportunity began developing separate guidelines for Alaska and Hawaii in 1966.

Unlike the poverty thresholds, the poverty guidelines do not distinguish income needs by age. The poverty guidelines are designated by the year in which they are issued. For instance, the guidelines issued in February 2003 are designated the 2003 poverty guidelines, even though they reflect price changes through the calendar year 2002. Therefore, they are approximately equal to the Census Bureau poverty thresholds for the year 2002.[4]

Recent Changes in the Number and Rate of Poverty

The 1990's economic boom helped to reverse some of the upward poverty trends of the late 1980's and early 1990's. The nation as a whole experienced a decline in poverty every year from 1992-2000.[5] The most dramatic change occurred in high poverty neighborhoods, where poverty rates are 40 percent or higher. During the 1990s' the number of people living in high poverty neighborhoods declined by 24 percent, or 2.5 million people. This change marked a turnaround from the period from 1970-1990 when the number of people living in high poverty areas doubled.[6] Unfortunately, after such a successful decade of decreasing poverty, increases were apparent in 2001, reflecting the recession that hit from March to November of that same year. The poverty rate rose from 11.3 in 2000 to 11.7 in 2001. Likewise, the number of people living in poverty also rose from 31.6 million to 32.9 million (see figure 4.1).[7] Some are concerned that the gains of the 1990's could be quickly lost if jobs and other economic opportunities are not restored, especially for low income families.[8] Recent reports from the Census Bureau's new *American Community Survey*, indicated a continued rise in poverty for 2002 to 12.4 percent.[9]

Figure 4.1

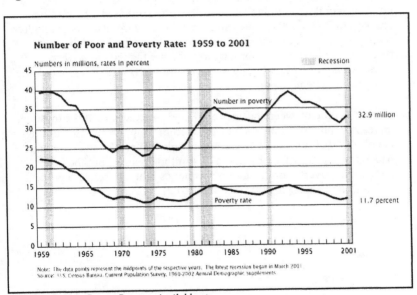

Source: U.S. Census Bureau; Available at:
http://www.census.gov/hhes/poverty/poverty01/pov01cht.gif

Risk of poverty by age

When we examine poverty in the U.S. by age we find that children are the ones who suffer the most (see figure 4.2). The poverty rate of children under 18 years of age was 16.3 percent in 2001 representing 11.7 million children. This rate and number was unchanged from 2000. While children make up 25.6 percent of the population, they account for 35.7 percent of the poor. Children under the age of 6 are the most vulnerable with a poverty rate of 18.2 percent in 2001, unchanged from 2000. Children under 6 living in single female-headed families are most at risk, with a poverty rate of 48.9 percent, or five times the rate of children living in married-couple families (9.2%).[10] What is most disturbing about the change in poverty rates for children is that the number of children living in extreme poverty increased by 5 million children to 7% in 2001, representing a 17% increase. Parents of children living in extreme poverty have an income of half the federal poverty threshold.[11] For example, for a family of three the federal poverty threshold is $14,072. A family of three earning $7,036 or less would be considered extremely poor.

People between the ages of 18 and 64 experienced the most net increase in poverty from 2000 to 2001, from 9.6 percent (16.7 million people) to 10.1 percent (17.8 million people). Those 65 and older also had a poverty rate of 10.1 percent (3.4 million people) but the net increase in poverty for this group was only slight, up from 9.9 percent (3.3 million people) in 2000 (see figure 4.2).[12]

Figure 4.2

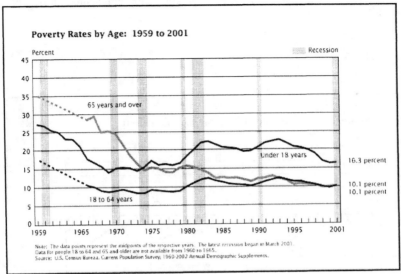

Source: U.S. Census Bureau; Available at:
http://www.census.gov/hhes/poverty/poverty01/povage01cht.gif

Risk of poverty by race

With the exception of Hispanics, all races showed increases in poverty from 2000-2001 (see figure 4.3). The White population poverty rate increased from 9.5 to 9.9 percent while the Black poverty rate increased from 22.5 to 22.7 percent; however, this change was not a statistically significant change for Blacks. It is important to note however that Blacks continue to experience one of the highest levels of poverty among all races, more than double that of the White population. Close behind is the Hispanic population with a poverty rate of 21.4 that remained constant from 2000. The highest poverty rate was among American Indians and Alaska Natives with a three year average (1999-2001) of 24.5 percent. A three year average is used to estimate poverty among Native Indians and Alaskans because the Current Population

Survey sample used by the U.S. Census Bureau to calculate poverty rates is not large enough to accurately calculate poverty rates within a one year period for this small segment of the population (not represented on figure 4.3).[13]

Figure 4.3

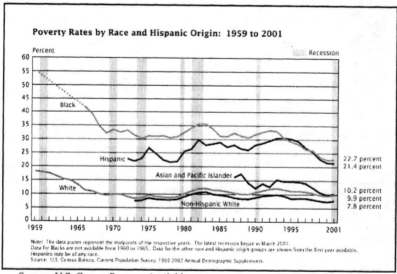

Source: U.S. Census Bureau; Available at:
http://www.census.gov/hhes/poverty/poverty01/povrac01cht.gif

Families in Poverty

Families experienced an increase in poverty in 2001 of 9.2 percent, up from a 26 year low rate of 8.7 percent in 2000. Asian and Pacific Islander families showed no change staying constant at 7.8 percent, while Black families were hit hardest with a 6.8 percent of change from 19.3 percent in 2000 to 20.7 percent in 2001. Hispanic families had only a slight increase from 19.2 to 19.4 percent, while

68

White families had a 4.1 percent increase in poverty (see table 4.3).[14]
Estimates from the *American Community Survey* (U.S. Census Bureau)
indicate an increase of family poverty to 10.2 percent for 2002.[15]

Table 4.3: Poverty Rates for Families by Race
2000-2001

Family Race	Poverty Rates: 2000	2001	% of Change
All Families	8.7%	9.2%	5.4%
Asian/Pacific Islander Families	7.8	7.8	0.0
White Families	7.1	7.4	4.1
Hispanic Families	19.2	19.4	1.0
Black Families	19.3	20.7	6.8

Source: U.S. Census Bureau Current Population Survey,
2002 Annual Demographic Supplement

Married-couple families were the most economically secure in
2001 with a poverty rate of 5.7 percent, while female-headed families
with no husband present had the most difficult economic struggles,
experiencing a poverty rate of 28.6 percent. When no workers were
present in the female-headed household, the poverty rate soared to 70.2
percent. Male-headed households with no wife present had the second
highest poverty rates in 2001 at 13.6 percent This rate increased to 48
percent when no worker was present in the home (see figure 4.4). Having
one worker in the home decreased poverty rates dramatically for all
family types.[16]

Figure 4.4

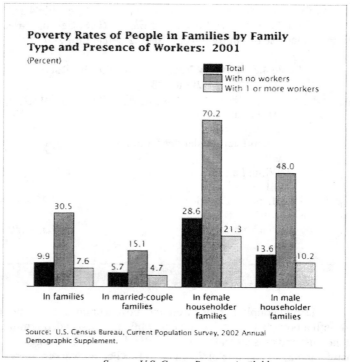

Source: U.S. Census Bureau: Available at:
http://www.census.gov/hhes/poverty/poverty01/povtyp01cht.gif

The intersection of family structure and race: Impact on poverty

The interaction of family type and race had devastating impacts for some families. For instance, single female-headed families had poverty rates from 25.4 percent (when all races were counted) to as high as 37 percent (Hispanic only) when isolating single female-headed families by race (see table 4.4). Most all families experienced an increase in poverty from 2000 to 2001 regardless of family type. There were two exceptions. Hispanic families of married-couples had a decrease in poverty from 14.2 percent in 2000 to 13.8 percent in 2001. Asian and

Pacific Islander families had the most significant decline in poverty. Single female-headed Asian and Pacific Islander families reduced their poverty from 22.2 percent in 2000 to 14.6 percent in 2001. Single male-headed families had the greatest increase in poverty from 11.3 percent in 2000 to 13.1% in 2001. The single male-headed families hit the hardest were Asian and Pacific Islanders (5.4% to 9.1%); Hispanics (13.6% to 17%); and Blacks (16.3% to 19.4%) (see table 4.4).[17]

Table 4.4: Poverty Rates by Family Type and Race (2000-2001)

Race Family Type	All		White		Black		Hispanic		Asian/Pacific Islander	
	2000	2001	2000	2001	2000	2001	2000	2001	2000	2001
Married-couples	4.7%	4.9%	4.4%	4.5%	6.3%	7.8%	14.2%	13.8%	5.9%	6.6%
Single Female Headed	25.4	26.4	21.2	22.4	34.3	35.2	36.4	37	22.2	14.6
Single Male Headed	11.3	13.1	10.1	11.7	16.3	19.4	13.6	17	5.4	9.1

Source: U.S. Census Bureau Current Population Survey, 2002 Annual Demographic Supplement

Homelessness in the Land of Plenty

Despite the economic boom of the 1990's, homelessness grew.[18] Those who benefited from the economic growth during the 1990's tended to be high wage earners. Lower income earners actually lost wages.[19] In 2001, homelessness touched the lives of 2.3-3.5 million adults and children in the U.S., or one out of every hundred Americans. On any given night, 700,000 to 800,000 people were homeless. Slightly more than a third were families, two thirds were single adults, and twenty-two percent were children.[20] The current annual figures on homelessness represent about one percent of the U.S. population, but about 10% of the poor, those most vulnerable to homelessness. It is estimated that between 5-10% of poor people experience homelessness over the course of a given year.[21]

Homeless families

In 2001, half of those who experienced homelessness were single adults, half the homeless were members of family units, and about 38 percent are children.[22] In 2002, families made up 41% of the urban homeless population, representing a 5% increase in just two years.[23] In rural communities, research indicates that single mothers and children make up a larger portion of the homeless than is found in cities.[24] The most frequently cited reason for families becoming homeless is a housing crisis. Most families have other service needs as well, but these needs are best met when the family is in permanent housing. The major needs that homeless families report were:

- Help finding a job;
- Help finding affordable housing; and
- Financial help in paying for housing.

While most families identify their most pressing needs to be housing and paying for housing, when ask what services they actually received, only 20 percent said that they received help finding housing.[25]

Substance abuse, mental illness, and homelessness

The news media often depicts the homeless population as mentally ill and drug abusing individuals, but this image is misleading. While it is true that the mentally ill and substance abusers are overrepresented within the homeless population, they are not the majority of the homeless. Homeless persons with severe or persistent mental illness make up only 22% of the homeless population.[26]

The relationship between addiction and homelessness is complex and not fully understood; however, many non-poor addicts never experience homelessness. Addicts who are poor are particularly at risk for becoming homeless. It is difficult to estimate the number of homeless who are addicts, but the U.S. Conference of Mayors national survey of cities reported 34% of the homeless in sample cities were substance abusers.[27] The disproportionate number of mentally ill and substance abusers who are homeless has been linked to the insufficient and declining stock of supportive housing and treatment services.[28]

Ending homelessness

Over the last two decades, over $12 billion in federal funds and billions more of state funds has been spent on the problem of homelessness, but the problem has persisted, and even grown. While the system of caring for the homeless has expanded, the root causes, as understood by homeless advocates, have yet to be addressed. These root causes include safe, available, and affordable housing, jobs that provide living wages with health care benefits, and strong social service support networks, especially for the homeless who also suffer from disabilities.[29]

President Bush's Homeless Agenda

President Bush's major concern with homelessness has been with what has termed the 'chronic homeless,' and he has pledged to end chronic homelessness in ten years through a new Samaritan Initiative. The chronically homeless are defined as a sub-population who often have an addiction problem, or suffer from a disabling physical or mental illness. Research suggests that this group consist of approximately 150,000 people who are homeless for extended periods of time or

74

experience multiple episodes of homelessness; and, that while the chronically homeless comprise roughly 10 percent of the homeless population, they consume more than one-half of all homeless services because their needs are not comprehensively addressed.[30] Homeless advocates have voiced concerns about the Bush Administration's focus on chronic homelessness, because they claim that it 1) pathologizies and stigmatizes the homeless; and, 2) misrepresent the causes of homelessness as mental illness and substance abuse, and ignores the structural causes of homelessness, such as low wages and lack of affordable housing, that are the real causes of homelessness for most people who experience homelessness.[31]

To achieve the goal of ending chronic homelessness in a decade, homeless advocates estimate that approximately 150,000 new units of permanent supportive housing will need to be created. Supportive services include mental health and substance abuse counseling, employment training, health care, and case management. [32] President Bush has requested $50 million in funding for his new Samaritan Initiative for FY 2004.[33]

Federal homeless programs and funding levels

The major homeless assistance programs exist across five federal agencies; the Veterans Administration, Housing and Urban Development (HUD), the Labor Department, Health and Human Services (HHS), and the Department of Education; however, HUD provides more direct funding for homeless organizations than any other agency. In fiscal year (FY) 2004, President Bush requested $31.3 billion for HUD programs effecting homeless populations. This was slightly more than was funded for the 2003 budget ($31.47 billion). About $1.3 billion of homeless funds are for Homeless Assistance Grants that, until recent years, local communities could spend in accordance with local needs and priorities. In the last five years, Congress has required that 30% of these funds be spend on permanent housing for people with disabilities, including mental illness and substance abuse. This caused concern among local providers and homeless advocates, because it did not allow local experts to set local spending priorities. Since 2002, Congress has provided separate line item for permanent housing funds which prevents drawing

75

funds away from the Homeless Assistance Grants, and returned local decision-making about how to spend the funds to local communities.[34]

   HUD McKinney-Vento Homeless Assistance Programs. In 1987, Congress enacted the Stewart B. McKinney Homeless Assistance Act in response to the homelessness crisis that had emerged in the 1980s. The act was reauthorized in 2000, and renamed the McKinney-Vento Act. The act authorizes funds for a small set of federal homeless assistance programs, including four administered by HUD. Collectively, these programs are known as *HUD McKinney-Vento Homeless Assistance Programs,* and provide rent assistance, funds for building and maintaining homeless shelters, supportive services, and innovative and alternative housing (see table 4.5).[35]

Table 4.5: HUD McKinney-Vento Homeless Assistance Programs

Program Name	Program Description
Emergency Shelter Grants (ESG):	Provides states and communities with formula based federal funds for renovation, rehabilitation, or conversion of buildings for use as emergency shelters or transitional housing for people experiencing homelessness.
Section 8 Moderate Rehabilitation for Single Room Occupancy Dwellings for Homeless Individuals (SRO)	These funds are used to provide rental assistance for homeless individuals and are awarded to local agencies through a competitive process.
Shelter Plus Care (S+C)	Funds are awarded on a competitive basis to states, communities, public and Indian housing agencies, and nonprofit organizations to provide rental assistance, together with supportive services funded from a source other than this program, to homeless people with disabilities.
Supportive Housing Program (SHP)	Funds are awarded on a competitive basis to states, communities, and nonprofit organizations to finance transitional housing, permanent supportive housing, supportive services, innovative and alternative housing, and safe havens.

Source: National Coalition for the Homeless, March, 2002

In FY 2002, Congress appropriated $1.123 billion for HUD McKinney-Vento programs, including $100 million for Shelter Plus Care (S+C) renewals. The McKinney-Vento programs funds over 5,000 projects, serves over 614,000 homeless individuals in over 3,025 cities and counties across the nation. The McKinney-Vento programs were due for reauthorization in 2002, but so far no bill has been introduced and authorized.[36] There is agreement in Congress that these programs should be consolidated with other homeless programs. The Community Partnership to End Homelessness Act was introduced in 2002 with bipartisan support and focused on consolidating the homeless programs, but did not get enacted.[37]

Table 4.6: Summary of Bringing Home America Act [H.R. 2897]

Provisions	Description	Changes in Current Law/Programs
Establishes the National Affordable Housing Trust Fund	Provides funding for specified housing and related programs; and, authorizes appropriations for specified housing and related programs	Amends the Cranston-Gonzalez National Affordable Housing Act
Establishes the Federal Homelessness to Housing Mutual Mortgage Association (Hollie May)	Provides housing and homeownership opportunities for the homeless in cooperative housing associations	
Provide for the use of surplus Federal property to assist the homeless; and revise and consolidate specified homeless assistance programs		Amends the McKinney-Vento Homeless Assistance Act to: (1)
Establishes in the Treasury the Emergency Rent Relief Fund	Exempts work performed in public housing from consideration as income under specified housing programs	
Sets forth conditions for postal delivery service for the homeless		
Authorizes grants for public housing police forces		
Establish a temporary ex-offender low-income	Expresses the sense of Congress against local ordinances that	Amends the Internal Revenue Code

77

housing credit; (2) limit mortgage interest deductions; and (3) repeal the exclusion of gain on a principal residence sale	disadvantage the homeless.	
Authorizes appropriations for specified health and homeless programs	Expresses the sense of Congress that every person in the United States should have access to affordable and comprehensive medical care	Expands Medicaid
Expands services for substance abuse, mental health services for the homeless	Require the establishment of Federal plans on addiction, mental illness, HIV/AIDS, and homelessness and provides grants for treatment	Amends the Public Health Service Act; revise the projects for assistance in transition from homelessness (PATH) program; revise the Ryan White Comprehensive AIDS Resources Emergency Act of 1990
Authorizes a Department of Labor apprenticeship program for working people experiencing homelessness;	Expresses the sense of the Congress regarding the right to a living; authorizes grants for a homebuild program for affordable housing construction and apprenticeship; sets forth day laborer and temporary worker employment and related provisions wage or similar benefits.	Amends the Cranston-Gonzalez National Affordable Housing Act
Increase income security for the homeless	Require supplemental security income (SSI) and old age, survivors, and disability insurance (OASDI) outreach programs for the homeless; and (2) increase SSI asset limits, and provide presumptive eligibility for persons experiencing or at risk of homelessness.	Amends the Social Security Act

Source: THOMAS, Legislative Information on the Internet. Available at http://thomas.loc.gov

In July, 2003 an important piece of legislation was introduced in the House. The Brining Home America Act [H.R. 2897] was introduced by Rep. Julia Carson (IN). The bill calls for sweeping changes in housing, work, IRS, health care, and income assistance programs, and expresses to Congress the principles of housing, living wages, and health care as human rights. Table 4.6 summarizes the provisions of the bill and the existing laws that would require amendment as a result of the

Bringing Home America Act being enacted. This bill has garnered swift and tremendous support from homeless advocates across the country.[38]

Housing for the poor

According to the National Coalition for the Homeless, over 14.4 million families have critical housing needs, largely due to the simultaneous decline in low-rent units, and the increase in the number of low-income renters over the past 20 years. The coalition estimates that it would take an annual production of 250,000 low-income housing units for more than 20 years to close the affordable housing gap. In spite of the growing housing gap for the poor, the White House requests for Section 8 vouchers to assist the poor in obtaining safe, affordable housing, has actually declined over the years. In 1976, the Ford Administration requested over 400,000 Section 8 vouchers. In 2003, President Bush requested just 34,000.[37] Only about one-third of poor renter households receive federal housing assistance.[39]

Approximately 42% of the homeless are in the work force, but they cannot afford housing.[40] According to housing advocates, it would take an hourly wage of $15.21 (housing wage) to afford the rent on a two bedroom apartment nationally-weighted at the Fair Market Rent (FMR). The housing wage is the amount a person will have to earn in order to pay the FMR without spending more that 30% of their income (30% is the federal recommendations for housing cost/income ratio). The Fair Market Rent (FMR) is the U.S. Department of Housing and Urban Development's (HUD) best estimate of what a person will have to pay to rent standard quality housing locally. The increase in the housing wage to $15.21 in 2003 represented a 37% increase in the housing wage from the 1999 level of $11.08. The current housing wage is nearly three times the federal minimum wage, and double the highest state minimum wage.[41]

Proposed changes in federal housing programs

HOPE VI . HUD's HOPE VI program was intended to help public housing agencies around the country to rehabilitate and reconstruct public housing units, and to provide supportive community services for residents; thus lifting those most severely distressed out of poverty. That has not been the outcome for many communities. More units have been demolished that new ones constructed, resulting in a net loss in the number of affordable low-income housing units.[42] Funded at over $550 million for the past two years, President Bush has proposed no funding for this program in his 2004 budget requests.[43]

Housing Choice Voucher Program. The Section 8 Housing Choice Voucher program and the Section 8 project-based housing subsidy program are two of HUD's major rentals housing programs, helping three million low-income households pay the rent on privately owned apartments. The Bush Administration has proposed to revamp the Section 8 Housing Choice Voucher Program and has introduced legislation in the House (H.R. 1841) and Senate (S. 947)[44] for the creation of Housing Assistance for Needy Families (HANF) program. This legislation would convert the voucher program to a state-run block grant. Project-based assistance would continue to be administered by HUD. The Administration's intention is to better assist low-income households to locate decent, safe, and affordable housing by giving states more latitude to tailor programs to the needs of particular communities. For example, in states that have large cities with expensive rental housing, a higher rent ceiling could be allowed in those areas.[45] Instead of funding a specific number of vouchers, as is done under the current program, states could serve an unspecified number of people as long as they did not serve fewer than were served by the Housing Choice Voucher program as of September 30, 2004.[46]

ENDNOTES

1. Much of the information in this section is taken from *Poverty in the United States: 2001* by Bernadette D. Proctor and Joseph Dalaker, Current Population Reports, Consumer Income, September, 2002 Washington DC: U.S. Census Bureau, U.S. Department of Commerce.
2. Bernadette D. Proctor and Joseph Dalaker, *Poverty in the United States: 2001,* U.S. Census Bureau, Current Population Reports, Consumer Income, P60-219 (Washington DC: U.S. Government Printing Office. 2002), p. 5.

3. U. S. Department of Health and Human Services, *The 2003 HHS Poverty Guidelines,* http://aspe.hhs.gov/poverty/03poverty.htm Accessed September 9, 2003.

4. Ibid.

5. Bernadette D. Proctor and Joseph Dalaker, *Poverty in the United States: 2001,* U.S. Census Bureau, Current Population Reports, Consumer Income, P60-219 (Washington DC: U.S. Government Printing Office. 2002), p. 2.

6. Paul A. Jargowsky, *Stunning Progress, Hidden Problems: The Dramatic Decline in Concentrated Poverty in the 1990s,* (Washington DC: The Brookings Institution, May, 2003).

7. Bernadette D. Proctor and Joseph Dalaker, *Poverty in the United States: 2001,* U.S. Census Bureau, Current Population Reports, Consumer Income, P60-219 (Washington DC: U.S. Government Printing Office. 2002), p. 3-4.

8. Paul A. Jargowsky, *Stunning Progress, Hidden Problems: The Dramatic Decline in Concentrated Poverty in the 1990s,* (Washington DC: The Brookings Institution, May, 2003).

9. American Community Survey Profile Changes 2001-2202. U.S. Census Bureau. http://www.census.gov/acs/www/Products/Profiles/Chg/2002/01 02/Tabular/010/01000US3.htm Accessed September 9, 2003.

10. Bernadette D. Proctor and Joseph Dalaker, *Poverty in the United States: 2001,* U.S. Census Bureau, Current Population Reports, Consumer Income, P60-219 (Washington DC: U.S. Government Printing Office. 2002), p. 3-4.

11. National Center for Children in Poverty, "Low-Income Children in the United States, 2003," Columbia University Mailman School of Public Health, New York, NY. http://www.nccp.org/pub_cpf03.html Accessed September 9, 2003.

12. Bernadette D. Proctor and Joseph Dalaker, *Poverty in the United States: 2001,* U.S. Census Bureau, Current Population Reports, Consumer Income, P60-219 (Washington DC: U.S. Government Printing Office. 2002), p. 3-4.

13. Ibid., pp. 4 & 6.

14. Ibid., pp. 3 & 6.

15. American Community Survey Profile Changes 2001-2202. U.S. Census Bureau.

http://www.census.gov/acs/www/Products/Profiles/Chg/2002/01
02/Tabular/010/01000US3.htm Accessed September 10, 2003.
16. Bernadette D. Proctor and Joseph Dalaker, *Poverty in the United States: 2001,* U.S. Census Bureau, Current Population Reports, Consumer Income, P60-219 (Washington DC: U.S. Government Printing Office. 2002), p. 3, 7-8.
17. Ibid., p. 3.
18. Martha Burt, *What will it Take to End Homelessness?* (Washington DC: The Urban Institute, October 1, 2001).
19. U.S. Census Bureau, "Money income in the United States: 2001," *Current Population Reports: Consumer Income,* (Washington DC: Department of Commerce).
20. Martha Burt, *America's Homeless II: Populations and Services* (Washington DC: Urban Institute, 2000).
21. Martha Burt, *What will it Take to End Homelessness?* (Washington DC: The Urban Institute, October 1, 2001).
22. Martha Burt, *America's Homeless II: Populations and Services* (Washington DC: Urban Institute, 2000).
23. U.S. conference of Mayors, *A Status Report on Hunger and Homelessness in America's Cities: 2002* (Washington DC: Author) www.usmayors.org Accessed September 10, 2003.
24. Yvonne Vissing, *Out of Sight, Out of Mind: Homeless Children and Families in Small Town America,* (Lexington, KY: The University Press of Kentucky, 1996).
25. National Alliance to End Homelessness, *Annual Report 2001.* (Washington DC: Author) p.3.
http://www.naeh.org/pub/anreport2001.pdf Accessed September 10, 2003.
26. U.S. Conference of Mayors, *A Status Report on Hunger and Homelessness in America's Cities: 2001,* (Washington DC: Author).
27. U.S. Conference of Mayors, *A Status Report on Hunger and Homelessness in America's Cities: 1998* (Washington DC: Author, 1998).
28. National Coalition for the Homeless, *Why are People Homeless?* (Washington DC: Author, September, 2002).
29. National Alliance to End Homelessness, *Annual Report 2001.* (Washington DC: Author), p.3.

http://www.naeh.org/pub/anreport2001.pdf Accessed September 10, 2003.

30. U.S. Department of Housing and Urban Development, http://www.whitehouse.gov/news/usbudget/budget-fy2004/hud.html Accessed September 11, 2003.

31. National Coalition for the Homeless, *Poverty vs. Pathology: What's Chronic about Homelessness?* (Washington DC: Author). http://www.nationalhomeless.org/chronic/full.html Accessed September 11, 2003.

32. Policy Papers, *New Partnerships for Ending Homelessness: Housing, Service and Employment,* (National Alliance to End Homelessness, Corporation from Supportive Housing, & AIDS Housing of Washington, July 2003).

33. Office of Management and Budget, *Total Outlays for Grants to State and Local Governments by Function, Agency and Program: 1940-2008,* http://w3.access.gpo.gov/usbudget/index.html Accessed September 11, 2003.

34. Ibid.

35. National Coalition for the Homeless, *HUD McKinney-Vento Homeless Assistance Programs*, (Washington DC: Author, March, 2002), http://www.nationalhomeless.org/mckinney2001.html Accessed September 11,2003.

36. Ibid.

37. National Coalition for the Homeless, *People Need Affordable Housing,* (Washington DC: Author, July 2003) http://www.nationalhomeless.org/facts/housing.html Accessed September 11, 2003.

38. THOMAS, Legislative Information on the Internet. Available at *http://thomas.loc.gov/cgi-bin/bdquery/z?d108:HR02897:@@@L&summ2=m&* Accessed September 27, 2003.

39. National Coalition for the Homeless, *Why are People Homeless?* (Washington DC: Author, September, 2002).

40. National Coalition for the Homeless, *Welfare to What II,* (Washington DC: Author, 2001).

41. National Low Income Housing Coalition, *Out of Reach 2003: America's Housing Wage Climbs,* (Washington DC: Authors, 2003) http://www.nlihc.org/oor_current/ Accessed September 11,2003.

41. Child Welfare League of America, *Housing and Homelessness: Housing Solutions for Child Welfare Families,* (Washington DC: Author) http://www.cwla.org/programs/housing/ Accessed September 11, 2003

42. U.S. Department of Housing and Urban Development, http://www.whitehouse.gov/news/usbudget/budget-fy2004/hud.html Accessed September 11, 2003.

43. Thomas, Legislative Information on the Internet http://thomas.loc.gov/ Accessed September 11, 2003

44. U.S. Department of Housing and Urban Development, http://www.whitehouse.gov/news/usbudget/budget-fy2004/hud.html Accessed September 11, 2003.

45. Policy Papers, *New Partnerships for Ending Homelessness: Housing, Service and Employment,* (National Alliance to End Homelessness, Corporation from Supportive Housing, & AIDS Housing of Washington, July 2003).

SECTION FIVE

THE RISE IN UNEMPLOYMENT RATES AND THE EXHAUSTION OF UNEMPLOYMENT COMPENSATION INSURANCE BENEFITS

The 2001 Recession and the Rise in Unemployment

Since the recession began in March 2001, 3.3 million private sector jobs have disappeared, the largest sustained loss of jobs since the Great Depression. One point three million jobs have been lost since the official end of the recession November 2001.[1] Unemployment rates have swung from a high of 8.0% in January, 1993 to a low of 3.6% in October of 2000. The unemployment rate hovered between 3.6 and 3.7% until January 2001 when it started its incline again at 4.7% just preceding the official recession of March-November 2001. As the impact of the impression rippled throughout the country, unemployment rates continued to rise and jobs contracted across all industries, with manufacturing and information technology suffering the most. The unemployment rate peeked in January and July 2003 at 6.5%.[2] In August 2003, the unemployment rate started to decline again to 6.0% representing about 8.83 million people out of work (see figure 5.1).[3]

85

Figure 5.1

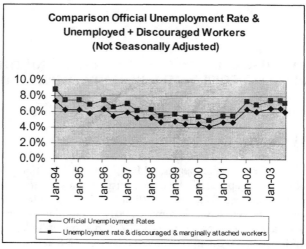

Source: Bureau of labor Statistics

When all women (16 and over) were assessed, women were more likely to be unemployed than men (6.2% and 5.9% respectively in August 2003).[4] However, when unemployment rates were seasonally adjusted, and adult women and men (age 20 and over) were compared, women faired better than men with an unemployment rate of 5.2% compared to 5.8% for adult men. Teenagers (16.6%) and people of color (Blacks 10.9%; Hispanic/Latino 7.8%) experienced much higher rates of unemployment that the adult and white (5.4%) segments of the population (see table 5.1).[5]

Table 5.1: Unemployment Rates by Selected Characteristics

Group	Unemployment Rate %
Adult Men	**5.8%**
Adult Women	**5.2**
Teenagers	**16.6**
Blacks	**10.9**
Hispanic/Latino	**7.8**

Source: Bureau of Labor Statistics; seasonally adjusted, August, 2003

The official unemployment rate counts only those workers who were unemployed and actively sought work within the four week period before the survey was conducted.[6] If other discouraged workers and those marginally attached to the work force are included in the unemployment rate, it increases by an average of 1 percentage point, or an additional 1.48 million people (see figure 5.1). Marginally attached workers are people who are currently not working and not looking for work, but say that they want work and are available for work and have actively sought work within the past year, but have stopped looking because they don't believe there are any jobs available.. Discouraged workers are a subset of marginally attached workers who give market-related reasons for not working, such as going to school.[7]

As the (unofficial) recession continued, people experienced longer periods of employment. In August, 2002, 1.8% of the unemployed had been unemployed for 15 weeks or long. By August 2003, that number had increased to 2.4%.[8] The average number of weeks people were without work increased from 16.3 weeks in August 2002 to 19 weeks in Augusts 2003.[9] Twenty-one point eight percent of the unemployed or 1.9 million workers were experiencing 6 months or more of unemployment in August 2003. In addition, approximately 3.5%-4% of the population was working in part-time jobs because they have been unable to find full-time work.[10] People were also taking on multiple jobs to make ends meet. In August 2003, 5.4% of workers were working 2 or more jobs, up from 5% in August 2002.[11]

States hit hardest by the recession tended to be in the South and in the West (see table 5.2), while those who faired the best tended to be in the Midwest, North and Northeast sections of the country (see table 5.2)[12] Most states provide a maximum benefit period of 26 weeks of unemployment compensation. Two exceptions, Massachusetts and Washington, provide 30 weeks of coverage.[13] The average benefit check was $200.58 in 1999 and $258.29 in 2002.[14] Maximum weekly benefits ranged from $190 in Alabama and Mississippi to $477 in Massachusetts in 2002.[15]

Table 5.2: States Most and Least Affected by the Recession
(July, 2003)

States with Highest Unemployment	Unemployment Rate (%)	States with Lowest Unemployment	Unemploy ment Rate (%)
Oregon	8.1	South Dakota	3.3
Alaska	7.9	North Dakota	3.6
Washington	7.5	Nebraska	3.9
Louisiana	7.4	Hawaii	4.0
Michigan	7.4	Virginia	4.0
Mississippi	7.2	Delaware	4.1
South Carolina	7.0	Vermont	4.1
West Virginia	6.8	New Hampshire	4.3
North Carolina	6.6	Iowa	4.6
Texas	6.6	Maryland	4.6
California	6.6	Minnesota	4.6
District of Columbia	6.5	Montana	4.7
Illinois	6.5	Maine	4.9

Source: Economic Policy Institute analysis of Bureau of Labor Statistics (seasonally adjusted)

Unemployment Compensation Claims

About 126 million individuals were covered by all UC Programs in 2002, representing 97 percent of all wage and salary workers and 89 percent of the civilian labor force.[16] Unemployment initial claims went from 15.5 million in 1999 to 21.1 million in 2002. The percentage of covered workers who had exhausted their unemployment benefits rose from 36.4 percent in 1999 to 42.9 percent in 2002[17] The insured unemployment rate, those workers who are unemployed and are covered under Unemployment Compensation rose from 2.1 percent in 2001 to 2.8 percent in 2002. Collectively, states are estimated to spend $41.6 billion on unemployment benefits in 2003 and $40.8 billion in 2004. States are expected to outspend unemployment tax collections in 2003 by $13.5 billion and $6.8 billion in 2004.[18] Federal spending on unemployment compensation rose from $21.4 billion in

1999 to \$50.6 billion in 2002[19] and is expected to reach \$56.3 billion in 2003.[20]

Legislation Enacted to Help Struggling Workers

Five pieces of federal legislation were passed that extended and/or expanded unemployment compensation (UC) benefits for unemployed workers between December 2000 and August 2002. Table 5.3 provides a summary of each act. In December, 2000 the Consolidated Appropriation Act, 2001 (P.L. 106-554) extended unemployment compensation benefits to Indiana tribes.[21] States that had federally recognized Indian tribes within their borders were to amend state and local laws to cover unemployed members of Indian Tribes. By 2003, most states had enacted the necessary state and local legislation needed to comply with the federal mandate.[22]

The Economic Growth and Tax Relief Reconciliation Act of 2001 (P.L. 107-16)[23] was signed into law in June 2001 and, among other things, reduced the Federal income tax on unemployment benefits from 15% down to 10%, enabling workers to have more money to spend on life necessities.[24] The intention of the law was to provide financial relief to unemployed workers while at the same time stimulate the economy with additional consumer power.

Table 5.3: Summary of Legislation to Help Unemployed Workers

Legislation	Summary of Unemployment Compensation Benefits	Signed into Law
Consolidated Appropriations Act, 2001	Extended unemployment compensation benefits to Indiana tribes	Dec. 21 2000 P.L. 106-554
Economic Growth and Tax Relief Reconciliation Act of	Reduced the Federal income tax on unemployment benefits from 15% down to 10%	June 7 2001 P.L.

2001 Jobs Creation and Worker Assistance Act of 2002	Extended unemployment compensation benefits for an additional 13 weeks for individuals who had exhausted their 26 weeks of regular UC coverage	107-16 March 9 2002 P.L. 107-147
To Extend the Period of Availability of Unemployment Assistance under the Robert T. Stafford Disaster Relief and Emergency Assistance Act in the Case of Victims of the Terrorist Attacks of September 11, 2001	Extended unemployment assistance from 26 to 39 weeks for workers who lost their jobs as a direct result of the 9/11 attacks	March 25 2002 P.L/ 107-154
Trade Act of 2002	Extended unemployment and training benefits to workers directly affected by increased imports or shifts in production in other countries to maximum of 104 weeks	August 6 2002 P.L. 107-210

Source: Loryn Lancaster & Anne Vogel, "Changes in Unemployment Insurance Legislation in 2002," Monthly Labor Review, January 2003, pp. 30-41

The "Job Creation and Worker Assistance Act of 2002" (P.L. 107-147) established the Temporary Extended Unemployment Compensation (TEUC) program. Effective March 10 through May 31, 2003, the act extended unemployment compensation benefits for an additional 13 weeks for individuals who had exhausted their 26 weeks of regular UC coverage. Workers in states experiencing high and/or rising unemployment rates could have their benefits extended an addition 13 weeks (for a total of 26 week extension). The benefits and administrative cost of P.L. 107-147 were paid for entirely with federal funds.[25] P.L. 107-147 also authorized a cash transfers of $8 billion from excess federal revenues in the Federal Unemployment Trust Fund to states. By law, when federal unemployment funds reach a statutory limit, excess funds are transferred to individual state accounts.[26] The transfers, known as the Reed Act transfers, were distributed on the bases of each state's share of the total taxable wage base under the Federal Unemployment Tax Act.[27] Most states used portions for the funds to extend benefits to the unemployed, and to create a reserve fund for future needs. One state, Vermont, used the funds to increase the amount of unemployment benefits.[28]

For workers who lost their jobs as a direct result of the 9/11 attacks, P.L. 107-154 extended unemployment assistance from 26 to 39 weeks authorized under the Robert T. Stafford Disaster Relief and Emergency Assistance, 1998. Under this law, workers in specified disaster areas who are not eligible for regular UC are entitled to receive disaster unemployment assistance.[29]

Finally, in August, 2002, the passage of the "Trade Act of 2002" (P.L. 107-210) implemented changes to the Trade Adjustment Assistance program, a federal program sponsored by the U.S. Department of Commerce. The program is a cost sharing federal assistance program that pays for half the cost of consultants or industry-specific experts for projects that improve a manufacturer's competitiveness.[30] The Trade Act of 2002 extended unemployment benefits to workers directly affected by increased imports or shifts in production in other countries, as well as workers secondarily affected by suppliers or producers servicing primary firms. Workers support while being retrained was increased from 52 to 78 weeks as well, making the maximum income support benefit 104 weeks of UC (78 weeks training support + 26 weeks UC).[31]

Impact of the Bush Administration's Economic Stimulus Package on Joblessness

The tax cut passed in May, 2003 by the Bush Administration, and put into effect in July 2003 was projected to increase job creation by 5.5 million jobs by the end of 2004, or 344,000 new jobs each month, starting in July 2003. However, results have been slow in coming. In August 2003, the jobs and growth plan fell 437,000 jobs short of the administration's projection,[32] with an overall job loss of 93,000 in August 2003.[33]

When unemployment remains high, it has the affect of lowering or depressing wages for those who do remain in the work force. The effect is evident in the current economy. A comparison of wages in the first half of 2003 to those the first half of 2002 shows that the growth of hourly wages has fallen when adjusted for inflation for all groups of earners. Wages have decline by 0.7%, 0.1%, and 1.0%, respectively, for low-, middle-, and high-wage workers.[34]

In response to the persistent unemployment, President Bush has requested that Congress pass legislation to establish 'Personal Reemployment Accounts' for unemployed workers. Under this proposed legislation, workers who face difficulty in reentering the workforce will receive up to $3,000 to use in their job search. The account can be used for job training, child care, transportation, or for relocation expenses for workers moving to a new city to accept a job. For those people who are able to find employment within a 13 week period, he or she will be able to keep the balance in the account as a reemployment bonus.[35]

Economic Outlook

The economic growth for 2003 is expected to be around 5% and the prediction for growth in 2004 is around 4%. But while the economic growth is good news, unemployment is expected to remain at around 6% throughout 2004, largely due to increases in productivity linked to increased uses of technology which allow companies to produce more goods with fewer people. It is expected that the stagnant unemployment rate will probably have a negative impact for the 2004 elections for the Republican Party who currently hold the majority of seats in the Senate and House of Representatives, and also for the re-election of President Bush.[36]

ENDNOTES

1. Economic Policy Institute, *Job Watch,* August, 2003, http://jobwatch.org/ Accessed September 17, 2003.

2. Bureau of Labor Statistics, Historical data *Unemployment Rates*, *Table A-11*(not seasonally adjusted), Washington DC. September 5, 2003.

3. Ibid.

4. Bureau of Labor Statistics, Historical Data, *Unemployment Rates*, Table A-1 (not seasonally adjusted), September 5, 2003.

5. Bureau of Labor Statistic, 'News' *Employment Situation Summary*, Washington DC, August, 2003.

6. Ibid.

7. Bureau of Labor Statistics, Historical Data, *Unemployment Rates*, (not seasonally adjusted), September 5, 2003.

8. Bureau of Labor Statistics, Historical Data, *Unemployment Rates, Table A-12* (not seasonally adjusted), September 5, 2003.

9. Bureau of Labor Statistics, Historical Data, *Unemployment Rates, Table A-9* (not seasonally adjusted), September 5, 2003.

10. Bureau of Labor Statistics, Historical Data, *Unemployment Rates, Table A-12* (not seasonally adjusted), September 5, 2003.

11. Bureau of Labor Statistics, Historical Data, *Unemployment Rates, Table A-13,* (not seasonally adjusted), September 5, 2003.

12. Economic Policy Institute, Job Watch : Tracking Jobs and Wages, *Unemployment Rate by State 28 Months after Start of Recession,* http://jobwatch.org/states/200309/unemployment_since_recessio n.pdf Accessed Sept. 17, 2003.

13. National Governors' Association, *Comparison State Unemployment Laws,* Washington DC. http://workforcesecurity.doleta.gov/unemploy/comparison.asp Accessed September 15, 2003.

14. Office of Budget and Management, *Unemployment Insurance Programs, Selected Data 1972-2002,* Historical Table B-45. Washington DC.

15. National Governors' Association, *Comparison State Unemployment Laws,* Washington DC. http://workforcesecurity.doleta.gov/unemploy/comparison.asp Accessed September 15, 2003.

16. Bureau of Labor Statistics, *Summary Data Tables,* U.S. Department of Labor, Washington DC.

17. Bureau of Labor Statistics, *UI Benefit Information,* U.S. Department of Labor, Washington DC

http://www.ows.doleta.gov/unemploy/content/data_stats/datasu
m99/4thqtr/benefits.asp Accessed September 19, 2003.

18. U.S. Department of Labor, Employment and Training
    Administration, Office of Workforce Security, *Data Summary*,
    Washington DC,
    http://workforcesecurity.doleta.gov/unemploy/content/midfy200
    4/home.asp   Accessed September 18, 2003.

19. Congressional Budget Office, *Historical Budget Data, Table 9*,
    Washington DC,
    http://www.cbo.gov/showdoc.cfm?index=1821&sequence=0
    Accessed September 15, 2003.

20. Office of Management and Budget, *Budget of the United States
    Government, Historical Tables*, Table 3.2, Washington DC.
    http://w3.access.gpo.gov/usbudget/fy2004/pdf/hist.pdf Accessed
    September 12, 2003.

21. THOMAS, Legislative Information on the Internet,
    www.thomas.loc.gov Accessed Sept. 17, 2003.

22. Loryn Lancaster & Anne Vogel, "Changes in Unemployment
    Insurance Legislation in 2002," *Monthly Labor Review*, January
    2003, pp. 30-41.

23. THOMAS, Legislative Information on the Internet,
    www.thomas.loc.gov Accessed Sept. 17, 2003.

24. Loryn Lancaster & Anne Vogel, "Changes in Unemployment
    Insurance Legislation in 2002," *Monthly Labor Review*, January
    2003, pp. 30-41.

25. Ibid., p. 30.

26. General Accounting Office, *States' use of the 2002 Reed Act
    Distribution*, Briefing GOA-03-496, Washington DC, February
    24, 2003.

27. National Governors' Association, Center for Best Practices,
    *Unemployment Compensation Provision and Related Issues,
    H.R. 3090, the Job Creation and Worker Assistance Act of 2002
    (Economic Stimulus Package Enacted March 9, 2002)*,
    Washington DC. p. 3.

28. General Accounting Office, *States' use of the 2002 Reed Act
    Distribution*, Briefing GOA-03-496, Washington DC, February
    24, 2003.

29. Loryn Lancaster & Anne Vogel, "Changes in Unemployment Insurance Legislation in 2002," *Monthly Labor Review,* January 2003, pp. 30-41.

30. U.S. Department of Commerce, Trade Adjustment Assistance for Firms, Economic Development Administration, Washington DC. http://www.taacenters.org/ Accessed September 17, 2003.

31. Loryn Lancaster & Anne Vogel, "Changes in Unemployment Insurance Legislation in 2002," *Monthly Labor Review,* January 2003, pp. 30-41.

32. Economic Policy Institute, *Job Watch,* August, 2003, http://jobwatch.org/ Accessed September 17, 2003.

33. Bureau of Labor Statistic, 'News' *Employment Situation Summary,* Washington DC, August, 2003.

34. Economic Policy Institute, *Job Watch,* August, 2003, http://jobwatch.org/ Accessed September 17, 2003.

35. *President Bush Pushes for Personal Reemployment Accounts Legislation,*
Remarks by the President on Employment Training, Ernst Community Cultural Center, Northern Virginia Community College, Annandale, Virginia, June 17, 2003. http://www.whitehouse.gov/news/releases/2003/06/20030617-3.html Accessed September 19, 2003.

36. Edmund L. Andrews, "Rapid Growth Seen for U.S. Economy," *New York Times.com,* September 13, 2003.

SECTION SIX

CARING FOR FAMILIES THROUGH WELFARE REFORM: HOW WELL HAS IT WORKED?

Welfare Reform: How Well Has It Worked?

Welfare reform under the Personal Responsibility and Work Opportunity Reconciliation Act of 1996 (PRWORA) shifted public assistance from a system historically focused on income supports, to a system that emphasized economic self-sufficiency through employment.[1] The four main goals of Temporary Aid to Needy Families (TANF) were to:

> ➢ Provide assistance to needy families;
> ➢ End welfare dependency through job readiness, work, and marriage;
> ➢ Reduce out-of-wedlock pregnancies; and,
> ➢ Encourage the formation of two parent families[2]

In this section, we look at how well TANF policies have met policy goals since implementation began in 1996. Specific areas examined include, how states have structured their TANF programs, how states have spent their TANF funds, how welfare recipients have faired under welfare reform, and the most important issues under consideration as TANF is considered for reauthorization by Congress.

How Have States Structured Their TANF Programs?

The rules of welfare programming established under PRWORA gave great flexibility to states in implementing the new welfare laws. States were allowed to:

- Set eligibility limits and cash benefits;
- Set income supplements for working families;
- Offer additional incentives and sanctions;

96

- Spend TANF funds on other non-cash programs and services aimed at meeting TANF goals;
- Save TANF block grant funds for economic downturns;[3]
- Extend Transitional Medicaid beyond 12 months; and,
- Design new work and education programs.[4]

Most states have allowed maximum benefits for TANF participants, although maximum benefit levels have continued to decline with inflation in most states. Between 1994 and 2000, maximum benefits for a family of 3 declined more than inflation in 7 states, equal to inflation in 29 states, less than inflation in 12 states, and benefits actually increased in real terms in 3 states.[5] States have used a variety of strategies to meet the needs of the poor within the boundaries of the 1996 welfare reform law. Below is a summary of strategies and sanction that states have used to deliver TANF assistance:

- 43 states require work before 2 years;
- 20 states do not exempt parents whose youngest child is 6 months or older;
- 15 states enforce 100% of sanctions possible for the first offense;
- 20 states have time limits or rolling time limits of less than 5 years;[6]
- 22 states apply sanctions to food stamps and Medicaid;
- 47 states have changed earnings disregard policies;
- 16 states have adopted state earned income tax credits and enacted other policies to help TANF participants work;
- All states have adopted more generous auto asset limits;
- 44 states have increased total asset limits; and,
- 11 states have extended Transitional Medicaid eligibility beyond 12 months.[7]

How Have States Spent Their TANF Funding?

Between 1996 and 2000, TANF cash assistance caseloads fell by about 50%. This dramatic decline in caseloads freed up TANF funds.

TANF funding levels were established at $16.5 billion annually for six years under the 1996 welfare authorization bill.[8] Since 1997, states have increased spending on child care, and saved large portions of the TANF funds for future needs especially during periods of economic down turn such as those that began in March 2001 and continue now well into 2003.

States have progressively spent more on work supports as well (also referred to as non-assistance), but less on basic cash assistance. In 1997, states spent 73% or $13.9 billion of TANF funds (state and federal combined) on basic assistance. That was down to 37% ($9.4 billion) in 2002 (see figures 6.1 & 6.2).[9] At the same time, a category of spending entitled 'non-assistance' grew from 23 percent to 56 percent of expenditures between 1997 to 2002, respectively (see figures 6.1 & 6.2). Non-assistance refers to non-cash or in-kind assistance that supports TANF recipients in finding and keeping jobs, as well as supports for increasing recipient earnings, such as earned income tax credits. Other non-assistance work supports include, but are not limited to, child care, transportation, work subsidies, and 'other' work supports (see table 6.1). The total spending for non-assistance increased from $2.27 billion in 1997 to $8.8 billion in 2002. Table 6.1 shows a breakdown of how the non-assistance dollars were spent. The largest amount accounted for in non-assistance spending was for work activities and child care. However, large portions of the non-assistance funds (80% in 1997 and 45% in 2002) were spent on 'other' supports.[10] Very little information is available that accounts for how these large amounts of funds were expended.[11]

Figure 6.1: Combined Expenditures
of Federal Funds and State TANF
by Spending Categories in FY1997 through the Fourth Quarter

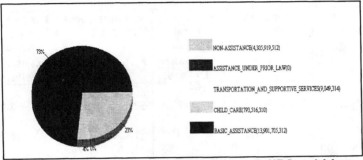

Source: U.S. Department of Health & Human Services; TANF financial data; Available at http://www.acf.dhhs.gov/programs/ofs/data/chart1_1997.html

Figure 6.2: Combined Expenditures Of Federal Funds
And State TANF
By Spending Categories In Fy2002 Through The Fourth Quarter

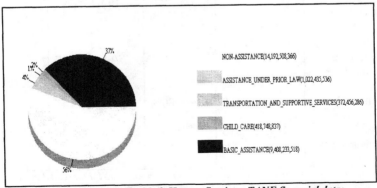

Source: U.S. Department of Health & Human Services; TANF financial data; Available at http://www.acf.dhhs.gov/programs/ofs/data/chart1_2002.html

Table 6.1: Combined Federal Funds Spent in FY1997 & FY2002 Expenditures On Non-Assistance in FY1997 & FY2002

Category of Spending	Amount Spent 1997	Percent of Total Non-Assistance Dollars	Amount Spent 2002	Percent of Total Non-Assistance Dollars
Work Related Activities	$ 450,361,452	20%	$2,120,690,902	24%
Child Care	43,195	<1%	1,496,951,451	17%
Transportation	0	0%	167,971,783	2%
Individual Development Accounts	0	0%	7,186,410	<1%
Refundable Tax Credits	0	0%	143,015,335	2%
Non-Recurring Short-Term Benefits	0	0%	143,479,567	2%
Non-Assistance Under Prior Law	0	0%	768,881,717	9%
'Other' Non-Assistance	1,816,953,169	80%	3,916,490,041	45%
Total Non-Assistance Spent	2,267,357,816	100%	8,764,669,206	100%

Source: U.S. Department of Health and Human Services; TANF Financial data, Table A; Available at   http://www.acf.dhhs.gov/programs/ofs/data/index.html

Child care spending

States' spending on child care grew dramatically between 1997 and 2000. This was largely due to states' ability to use TANF funds for child care assistance. Child care spending by states increased from $249 million in 1997 to $3.96 billion in 2000 (see figure 6.3). Federal law gives states the ability to use TANF funds for child care in two ways: 1) states may directly spend TANF funds on child care; and, 2) states may transfer up to 30% of TANF funds to their Child Care and Development Fund (CCDF). Child care funds transferred to CCDF peaked in 1999 at $2.58 billion and then began to decline. In 2002 the amount of TANF dollars transferred to CCDF was $1.93 billion (see figure 6.4). In 2002, 38 states used this transfer mechanism to fund child care for needy families, down from 40 states in 2001.[12]

Child care spending grew to be the largest single expenditure of TANF funds behind cash assistance, more than doubling the number of children receiving child care subsidies from 1996 to 2000. Even so, when child care spending reached its peak in 2000, only one out of seven eligible children was receiving child care assistance. In 2001, child care spending began to decline to $3.5 billion where it remained for 2002 (see figure 6.3).More cuts are projected for FY2003 and FY2004.[13] Cuts in child care spending have been linked to the down turn in the economy and subsequent state budget crises. As the economy has declined, states have had to increase spending on TANF as caseloads have begun to creep up again in some states.

Figure 6.3

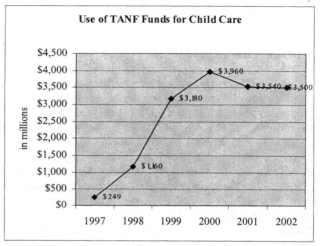

Use of TANF Funds for Child Care

Source: U.S. Department of Health & Human Services; Administration of
Children & Families; TANF Financial Data; Available at
http://www.acf.dhhs.gov/programs/ofs/data/index.htm l

Figure 6.4

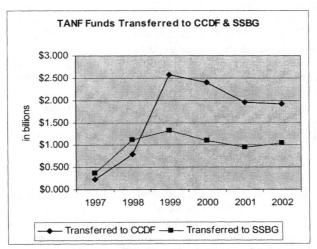

Source: U.S. Department of Health & Human Services; Administration Of Children & Families; TANF Financial Data; Available at http://www.acf.dhhs.gov/programs/ofs/data/index.html

Other spending

States are permitted to transfer up to 10% of TANF funds to their Social Service Block Grant (SSBG) for services to needy families.[14] The ability to transfer TANF funds to CCDF and SSBG allows states to provide services and benefits to low-income families, who do not qualify for traditional cash assistance payments.[15] Like other TANF spending trends, the amount of funds transferred to SSBG increased each year until 1999 were it peaked at $1.32 billion, and then began to decline in 2000. In 2001, funds transferred to SSBG had diminished to $934 million, but showed a slight increase again in 2002 to $1.03 billion (see figure 6.4).[16]

Relatively small amounts of TANF funds have been used for education and training. Less than 2% of TANF funds ($462 million) were used to enhance skills in 2002. This amount was a slight increase over 2000 spending levels. Similar amounts ($584 million) were spent on transportation and supportive services. Spending on pregnancy preventions programs has grown since 2000 when $102 million was spent to $726 million in 2002. Still, this represents a small percentage of total TANF funds (2.6%). Other modestly funded programs included Individual Development Accounts ($7.7 million in 2002), used to help low income families save money by matching funds when withdrawn for home ownership, education, or business start-ups,[17] and two-parent family formation programs ($284 million in 2002). Programs designed to put cash in the pockets of poor families have grown to $766 million in 2002. These include federal EICT credits and state funded tax credits.[18]

Spending forecast

In the past three years, the amount of TANF dollars expended by states exceeded the grant funds received,[19] making it necessary for states to pull upon their unobligated TANF balances or 'rainy day' funds. Between 2000 and 2002, the rainy day funds for states dropped from $3.2 billion to $2.7 billion. The large caseload declines experienced in the early years of TANF have slowed, and since the start of the recession, 29 states have reported caseload increases. For those states reporting a decrease in caseloads, the size of the decline has diminished significantly; however, nationally, caseloads continue to decline, but slowly (-1.9% 2002-2003) (see table 6.2).[20] States and welfare advocates have voiced concerns about the ability to maintain cash benefit and work supports at current levels if the economy continues to be depressed.[21] Many states have curtailed, or expect to cut services and cash benefits to TANF recipients in response to state budget crises, complicated by rising Medicaid cost, eroding tax bases, and federal fiscal pressures through mandates, such as Homeland security.[22]

TANF Program Outcomes

Overall, the caseloads declined a total of 51% since 1995 going from 4.59 million cases to 2.35 cases in 2000.[23] In terms of meeting the goal of decreasing dependency on public assistance, welfare reform appears to have been a success. However, some caution is warranted in assessing welfare reform policy outcomes. Welfare reform has largely taken place during the economic boom times of the 1990s when job opportunities expanded by 21 million jobs. It is probable that many of the declines in caseloads were in response to not only welfare reform policies, but also to the positive economic times. That having been said, however, it is also important to note that historically, before welfare reform, economic boom times did not result in dramatic decreases in caseloads.[24] The General Accounting Office concluded that the strong economy, changes in welfare policies, and other policies affecting low-wage earners all contributed to the increase in work among low-income single mothers, and the decline in TANF caseloads.[25] The needs of the poor need to continue to be closely monitored within the current economic downturns of 2001-2003 and beyond. This will be the true test of the success of welfare reform, not only in number of cases serviced or removed from the rolls, but also in the ability of welfare reform programs to provide necessary supports and assistance during periods of high unemployment, evaporating jobs, and declining wages.

For the past five years, TANF caseloads have consistently declined across the nation, however, the decline has lessened with each passing year, as would be expected. (see table 6.2).). In the face of a difficult economy, most states continue to report fluctuating caseloads, however, six states have reported a steady increase in caseloads between September 2002 – March 2003, and no states have reported a steady decline during the same reporting period.[26]

Table 6.2: Changes in TANF Caseloads 1997-2003

	Change in National TANF Caseload	# of States with Annual Caseload Declines > than 15 Percent
1997-1998	-20.1%	39
1998-1999	-16.9%	28
1999-2000	-14.6%	17
2000-2001	-6.9%	5
2001-2002	-2.2%	3
2002-2003	**-1.9%**	**2**

Source: Center for Law and Policy

Studies on TANF recipients who leave welfare show that about 75% work at some point after leaving, earning on average $7/hour. Less than half (43%) are receiving food stamps, 15% are using child care supports, and 50-85% are receiving Earned Income Tax Credits (EITC).[27] Food stamps participation rates have been in decline since 1994 but at an accelerated rate since the implementation of welfare reform in 1996. The decline in the use of this universal anti-poverty program has been linked to problems with assessing eligibility and benefits for the working poor and with ensuring that families leaving welfare for work continue to receive the food stamp benefits for which they are eligible.[28] Lack of child care supports are due to under-funding at state and federal levels, and not accessing EICT benefits has historically been understood as a lack of knowledge on the part of the poor regarding this benefit. On the positive side, research has shown that:

> ➢ About 2 million mothers are working who previously had been on welfare;
> ➢ Single mothers are earning more; and
> ➢ Child poverty has declined since 1996.[29]

For those leaving welfare, many continue to rely on government work supports such as food stamps, Medicaid, child care, and other forms of assistance.[30] Work supports included:

> ➢ Child care;
> ➢ Medicaid;
> ➢ State Children's Health Insurance Program (SCHIP);
> ➢ Food stamps;
> ➢ Child tax credit;
> ➢ Earned income tax credit; and,
> ➢ Housing

Work supports account for around $80 billion in annual benefits to the poor. The typical mother leaving welfare earns about $10,000 per year. In 1999, Congress expanded the benefit available to the working poor through the Earned Income Tax Credit (EITC) to a maximum benefit of $4000. This serves as a significant work support for single mothers leaving welfare. In addition, some states have instituted state level income tax credits for the working poor. The work supports of

EITC ($4000) and food stamps ($2000) increases her earnings to $16,000. Also, she and her children will be provided with Medicaid for at least a year (some states have extended this benefit beyond a year), after which her children are eligible for State Child Health Insurance Program (SCHIP) as long as the mother's income remains below $30,000.[31] While work supports have proven to be essential for moving single welfare mothers off welfare and into work, work support funds are limited and do not provide supports to all those who are eligible. For instance, only one in seven eligible children receive child care assistance,[32] and only about 25% of TANF recipients who qualify for housing assistance receive it. Many leaving welfare do not access supports that they are eligible for as they leave the welfare rolls.[33]

A study on the outcomes of TANF families leaving welfare in the Midwest found that most people who left welfare did go to work, but took jobs that were part-time or temporary, lasting only a few months. Thus, many families who have left welfare remain poor because of low earnings.[34] The major employer of TANF recipients is the service sector.[35]

Many of the problems that led families to welfare remain as barriers to work for TANF recipients. Health care problems, lack of education and skills, mental illness, substance abuse, disabilities, and, child care and transportation problems are the prominent barriers to work for those remaining on welfare. The Joyce Foundation study found that the more problems people faced, the less likely they were to work, and that those with the severest problems often left welfare involuntarily due to sanctions for not meeting program demands.[36] Clearly, as the public debate continues around issue of reauthorization, these issues need to addressed in terms of funding, spending priorities, and program development and flexibility, if those confronted with the most difficult barriers to work are to transition off welfare.

Other problems remain in assessing the successes and failures of TANF policies and programs. One serious problem is the difficulty in tracking TANF families after they leave welfare. For many, they fall through the research and evaluation cracks and it is unclear what becomes of them. Homeless advocates and homeless researchers claim that former welfare recipients are still out of work or earning poverty level wages and suffering from homelessness, hunger, and lack of adequate medical care.[37]

Two other goals of TANF were to decrease out-of-wedlock births, and to increase two-parent families. Gains have been made in the areas of family formation and reducing illegitimacy rates. Since 1991, teen births have steadily declined, and rates of illegitimacy for all ages have leveled off since the mid 1990's. There has been a slight increase in the number of children born to two parent families. While it is difficult to link these changes directly to welfare reform since many of the changes began before the 1996 reform act was passed, it is probable that the welfare debate and changes in law had some impact on illegitimacy rates.[38]

The Reauthorization of TANF

When the Personal Responsibility and Work Opportunity Reconciliation Act of 1996 (PRWORA) was enacted, it was authorized by Congress until 2002. Reauthorization legislation began being considered in 2002 during the 107th Congress, but agreement on a reauthorization bill did not occur. Much discussion has ensued throughout 2002 and into 2003 as reauthorization continues in process. The House passed the Personal Responsibility, Work, and Family Promotion Act of 2003 [H.R. 4] on February 13, 2003, and the bill was referred to the Senate committee September 10, 2003.[39] On February 14, 2003, Senate bill 5, the Compassion and Personal Responsibility Act, was introduced in the Senate where it has been read twice and referred to the Senate Finance Committee. Other reauthorization bills are also under consideration. Through debates, research, and testimonies among legislators, scholars, and advocates, general agreement on some issues about welfare reform reauthorization has occurred. Areas of general agreement among Democrats and Republicans include:

> Maintaining federal TANF block grant funding at the current level of $16.5 billion. Some advocates have argued for increases to keep up with inflation, and also because of the concerns of increased spending during the last two years of economic decline;

- There is agreement that given the need for child care, more funding needs to be appropriated for child care supports. Most of the bills being considered recommend increases in child care funding;
- Most legislators are in agreement with keeping the 5 year time limit on TANF benefits.[40]

Other reauthorization issues under discussion, but yet to be resolved by both parties include:

- Structuring bonuses for states based on pregnancy prevention programs and activities provided rather than on declines in illegitimacy rates;
- Mandate improved tracking of families by states as they leave welfare to ensure that they continue to receive work supports such as food stamps and Medicaid;
- Use of demonstration programs by states to more effectively serve poor families with multiple barriers to work;[41]
- Improve reporting requirements for states so that 'non-assistance' dollars can be better accounted for;[42]
- Improve performance outcome requirements for states in measuring TANF successes;
- Invest in effective education and training and allow education and training as part of the 'work activity' requirement under welfare reform;[43] and,
- Relaxing eligibility criteria for receiving foods stamps, and altering the procedures for delivering benefits to ensure that those who are eligible receive them.[44]

ENDNOTES

1. General Accounting Office, "Welfare Reform: Changing Labor Market and Fiscal Conditions," *Briefing to the Staff of the Senate Committee on Finance,* Washington DC, Many 13, 2003.

2. "The Politics of TANF Reauthorization," Welfare Reform and Beyond Initiative, Brookings Institution, Washington DC January 25, 2001.
   http://www.brook.edu/comm/transcripts/20010125_ii.htm Accessed September 19, 2003.

3. Ibid.

4. Margy Waller, "TANF Reauthorization: Options and Opportunities," *Presentation to the U.S. Conference of Mayors Annual Meeting*, June 15, Available at the Brookings Institution web page,
   2002http://www.brook.edu/es/urban/speeches/20020615waller.ht m Accessed September 21, 2003.

5. "The Politics of TANF Reauthorization," Welfare Reform and Beyond Initiative, Brookings Institution, Washington DC January 25, 2001.
   http://www.brook.edu/comm/transcripts/20010125_ii.htm Accessed September 19, 2003.

6. Margy Waller, "TANF Reauthorization: Options and Opportunities," *Presentation to the U.S. Conference of Mayors Annual Meeting*, June 15, Available at the Brookings Institution web page,
   2002http://www.brook.edu/es/urban/speeches/20020615waller.ht m Accessed September 21, 2003.

7. "The Politics of TANF Reauthorization," Welfare Reform and Beyond Initiative, Brookings Institution, Washington DC January 25, 2001.
   http://www.brook.edu/comm/transcripts/20010125_ii.htm Accessed September 19, 2003.

8. Jennifer Mezey and Brooke Richie, *Welfare Dollars no Longer an Increasing Source of Child Car Funding: Use of Funds in FY 2002 Unchanged from FY 2001, Down from FY 2000,* Center for Law and Social Policy, Washington DC August 6, 2003.

9. U.S. Department of Health and Human Services, Administration of Children and Families, *TANF Financial Data,* Washington

DC, Available at
http://www.acf.dhhs.gov/programs/ofa/tanfindex.htm Accessed
September 22 2003

10. Ibid.
11. Mark Greenberg and Elise Richer, *How States Used TANF and MOE Funds in FY 2002: The Picture from Federal Reporting,* Center for Law and Social Policy, Washington DC.
12. Jennifer Mezey and Brooke Richie, *Welfare Dollars no Longer an Increasing Source of Child Car Funding: Use of Funds in FY 2002 Unchanged from FY 2001, Down from FY 2000,* Center for Law and Social Policy, Washington DC August 6, 2003. p. 4.
13. Ibid., pp. 1-3.
14. Ibid., p. 2.
15. General Accounting Office, "Welfare Reform: Changing Labor Market and Fiscal Conditions," *Briefing to the Staff of the Senate Committee on Finance,* Washington DC, Many 13, 2003.
16. U.S. Department of Health and Human Services, Administration of Children and Families, *TANF Financial Data,* Washington DC, Available at
http://www.acf.dhhs.gov/programs/ofa/tanfindex.htm Accessed September 22, 2003
17. Michael Sherraden, Mark Schreiner, and Sondra Beverly, "Income, Institutions, and Saving Performance in Individual Development Accounts," *Economic Development Quarterly,* Vol. 17 No. 1 February, 2003 pp. 95-112.
18. Mark Greenberg and Elise Richer, *How States Used TANF and MOE Funds in FY 2002: The Picture from Federal Reporting,* Center for Law and Social Policy, Washington DC.
19. U.S. Department of Health and Human Services, Administration of Children and Families, *TANF Financial Data,* Washington DC, Available at
http://www.acf.dhhs.gov/programs/ofa/tanfindex.htm Accessed September 22, 2003
20. Elise Richer, Hedieh Rahmanou, and Mark Greenberg, *Welfare Caseloads in 27 States Decline in First Quarter of 2003: Most States Show Only Small Caseload Fluctuations,* Center for Law and Social Policy, Washington, DC July 18, 2003.
21. Jennifer Mezey and Brooke Richie, *Welfare Dollars no Longer an Increasing Source of Child Car Funding: Use of Funds in FY*

2002 Unchanged from FY 2001, Down from FY 2000, Center for Law and Social Policy, Washington DC August 6, 2003.

22. General Accounting Office, "Welfare Reform: Changing Labor Market and Fiscal Conditions," *Briefing to the Staff of the Senate Committee on Finance,* Washington DC, Many 13, 2003.

23. U.S. Department of Health and Human Services, Administration of Children and Families, Office of Family Assistance, *TANF REPORTS,* Washington DC, Available at http://www.acf.dhhs.gov/programs/ofa/tanfindex.htm Accessed September 22, 2003.

24. Joyce Foundation, *Welfare to Work: What Have we Learned,* Chicago, IL, March, 2002 available at http://www.joycefdn.org/pubs/pubsmain-fs.html Accessed September 23, 2003.

25. General Accounting Office, "Welfare Reform: Changing Labor Market and Fiscal Conditions," *Briefing to the Staff of the Senate Committee on Finance,* Washington DC, Many 13, 2003.

26. Elise Richer, Hedieh Rahmanou, and Mark Greenberg, *Welfare Caseloads in 27 States Decline in First Quarter of 2003: Most States Show Only Small Caseload Fluctuations,* Center for Law and Social Policy, Washington, DC July 18, 2003.

27. Margy Waller, "TANF Reauthorization: Options and Opportunities," *Presentation to the U.S. Conference of Mayors Annual Meeting,* June 15, Available at the Brookings Institution web page, 2002http://www.brook.edu/es/urban/speeches/20020615waller.htm Accessed September 21, 2003.

28. Michael Wiseman, "Food Stamps and Welfare Reform," *Welfare Reform and Beyond Policy Brief #19,* Brookings Institution, Washington DC, March, 2002.

29. Ron Haskins, "Welfare Reform: An Examination of Effects," *Testimony before House Committee on Education and the Workforce,* September 20, 2001. Transcript available at the Brookings Institution Web site http://www.brook.edu/views/testimony/haskins/20010920.htm Accessed September 24, 2003.

30. Joyce Foundation, *Welfare to Work: What Have we Learned,* Chicago, IL, March, 2002 available at

http://www.joycefdn.org/pubs/pubsmain-fs.html Accessed September 23, 2003.

31. Ron Haskins, "Welfare Reform: An Examination of Effects," *Testimony before House Committee on Education and the Workforce,* September 20, 2001. Transcript available at the Brookings Institution Web site http://www.brook.edu/views/testimony/haskins/20010920.htm Accessed September 24, 2003.

32. Jennifer Mezey and Brooke Richie, *Welfare Dollars no Longer an Increasing Source of Child Car Funding: Use of Funds in FY 2002 Unchanged from FY 2001, Down from FY 2000,* Center for Law and Social Policy, Washington DC August 6, 2003.

33. National Coalition for the Homeless, *People Need Livable Incomes,* Washington DC available at www.nationalhomeless.org/facts/income.html Accessed September 10, 2003.

34. Joyce Foundation, *Welfare to Work: What Have we Learned,* Chicago, IL, March, 2002 available at http://www.joycefdn.org/pubs/pubsmain-fs.html Accessed September 23, 2003.

35. General Accounting Office, "Welfare Reform: Changing Labor Market and Fiscal Conditions," *Briefing to the Staff of the Senate Committee on Finance,* Washington DC, Many 13, 2003.

36. Joyce Foundation, *Welfare to Work: What Have we Learned,* Chicago, IL, March, 2002 available at http://www.joycefdn.org/pubs/pubsmain-fs.html Accessed September 23, 2003.

37. National Coalition for the Homeless, "New National Survey of the Nation's Poor Challenges Success of Welfare Reform; Two Thirds Unemployed, High Percentage Hungry, Homeless and Lacking Insurance," *Press Release,* April 19, 2001, Washington DC.

38. Ron Haskins, "Welfare Reform: An Examination of Effects," *Testimony before House Committee on Education and the Workforce,* September 20, 2001. Transcript available at the Brookings Institution Web site http://www.brook.edu/views/testimony/haskins/20010920.htm Accessed September 24, 2003.

39. THOMAS *Legislative Information on the Internet*, Available at http://thomas.loc.gov/ Accessed September 23, 2003.

40. Margy Waller, "TANF Reauthorization: Options and Opportunities," *Presentation to the U.S. Conference of Mayors Annual Meeting*, June 15, Available at the Brookings Institution web page, 2002http://www.brook.edu/es/urban/speeches/20020615waller.ht m Accessed September 21, 2003.

41. Ron Haskins, "Welfare Reform: An Examination of Effects," *Testimony before House Committee on Education and the Workforce,* September 20, 2001. Transcript available at the Brookings Institution Web site http://www.brook.edu/views/testimony/haskins/20010920.htm Accessed September 24, 2003.

42. Mark Greenberg and Elise Richer, *How States Used TANF and MOE Funds in FY 2002: The Picture from Federal Reporting,* Center for Law and Social Policy, Washington DC.

43. National Coalition for the Homeless, "New National Survey of the Nation's Poor Challenges Success of Welfare Reform; Two Thirds Unemployed, High Percentage Hungry, Homeless and Lacking Insurance," *Press Release,* April 19, 2001, Washington DC.

44. Michael Wiseman, "Food Stamps and Welfare Reform," *Welfare Reform and Beyond Policy Brief #19,* Brookings Institution, Washington DC, March, 2002.

SECTION SEVEN

CARING FOR THE NATION'S NEEDY CHILDREN

In 2001, the number and percentage of female-headed families (with children) who were without work in an average week, yet had no welfare income, reached the highest point in the 26 years for which data are available. The increase in these families in 2001 (17 %) was by far the largest one-year increase on record. By the third quarter of 2001, the number of children in such jobless families with no TANF income had increased by 18% over the previous year to 626,000 children.[1] The sharp rise in the number of children living in homes with few resources accounts for the troubling increases in extreme child poverty that began to emerge in 2001 and continued in 2002.[2] The effects of poverty on children are extreme and many times irreversible. Children living in poverty are at greater risk for a multitude of unhealthy and undesirable outcomes. According to the Children's Defense Fund, children living in poverty are:

- 1.6 time more likely to die in infancy;
- 2.7 times more likely to have no regular source of health care;
- 2 times more likely to repeat a grade
- 3.4 times more likely to be expelled from school
- 3.5 times more likely to be a school drop-out (1 in 8 of all American children never graduate from H.S.)
- ½ as likely to finish college[3]

In America today, 12 million children are living in poverty and at risk for a multitude of problems. Eighty percent of children living in poverty live in working households.[4] Income, health, and education supports are required to grow healthy children into healthy and productive adults. In this section, we examine the health of government programs designed to guarantee the health and stability of children.

115

Implementation of the Children's Health Insurance Program

Next to income security, health care security is the single important items to insure health and security to our nation's children. In 2001, 41.2 million Americans were without health insurance, and 8.51 million were children.[5] The implementation of the Children's Health Insurance Program (CHIP) under the Balanced Budget Act of 1997 (Title XXI of the Social Security Act) has made significant headway in providing healthcare for children. CHIP, specifically targeted to serve uninsured children from low- and moderate-income families, gave states flexibility as to how they implemented CHIP.[6] Some (18) created a separate child health program; some (18) covered children through a combination of health programs, and others (14) expanded Medicaid to cover uninsured children. By the end of 2002, CHIP had served 5.32 million children.[7] Most states have set their eligibility for CHIP at 200% of federal poverty level (FPL), however one state, Arkansas set their eligibility standard at 100% of FPL. Other states were more generous. Three states (CT, MO, & VT) set participation eligibility at 300% FPL and New Jersey is at 350% FPL enabling them to capture more uninsured children in their state CHIP programs.[8]

Federal spending on CHIP has increased over the years as enrollment has grown from $1.44 billion in 1999 to $3.68 billion in 2002. Estimated expenditures for 2003 are $4.75 billion, however, President Bush calls for sever cuts in the CHIP budget for 2004, down to $2.66 billion (see figure 7.1).[9]

Figure 7.1

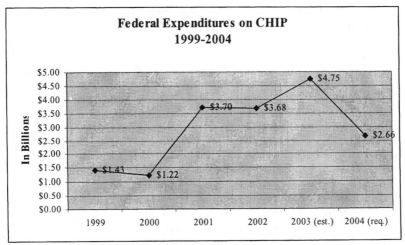

Source: U.S. Department of Health and Human Services; Available at http://www.hhs.gov/budget/docbudget.htm

Feeding our Children

Hunger continues to be a problem for some families and their children in the United States. Severe hunger has been shown to be a predictor of chronic illness. For preschooler, moderate hunger can significantly influence adverse health conditions and behavior problems.[10] In 2001, 11.5 million households were food insecure at some time during the year. "Food insecure" means that the families did not have access to enough food for healthy living for all household members. Some 3.5 million households experienced hunger. For the most part, children, especially younger children were shielded from hunger; however, 211,000 households reported food insecurity so severe that children in the household went hungry. Children with single mothers were three times more likely to experience hunger than children living in two parent families. From 1995-1999, food insecurity and hunger were declining in this country. As we entered the recession in 2001, food insecurity and hunger began to increase. From 1999-2001, the prevalence of food insecurity rose by 0.6% and the prevalence of hunger rose 0.3%.[11] Federal Nutrition Programs are the front line of defense for fighting hunger and food insecurity. Nutrition programs that have the greatest impact on children's nutrition are the Food Stamp Program, the Special Supplemental Nutrition Program for Women, Infants, & Children (WIC), and the Child Nutrition Programs.

The Food Stamp Program

The Food Stamp Program (FSP) is the nation's largest nutrition program and served 19 million people in 2002, and is expected to serve over 21 million in 2004 (see figure 7.2).[12] Twenty-five percent of the households who reported food insecurity in 2001 were receiving food stamps, and 28.5 percent who reported hunger used food stamps.[13] Throughout the mid to late 1990s the participation in food stamps declined, (see figure 7.2) most likely tied to rule changes in the 1996 welfare reform legislation. Rates of participation have begun to increase in resent years, however only 57% of those living in poverty receive food stamps.[14] Children make up 51percent of all food stamp users.[15]

Figure 7.2

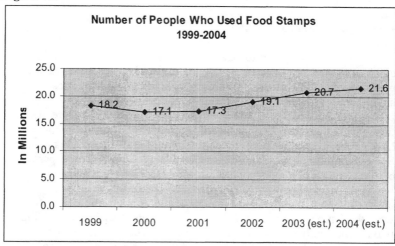

Source: U.S. Department of Agriculture; Available at
http://www.fns.usda.gov/pd/fssummar.htm

The average monthly food stamp benefit per person per month varies by state, and ranged from $62.69 in Kansas to $118.90 in Hawaii in 2002, with a state average of $79.55. In 2002, a family of four participating in the food stamp program received an average $318.20 in benefits each month. Average state benefit levels has grown from $72.21 in 1999 to $83.29 in 2003 (see figure 7.3).[16]

Figure 7.3

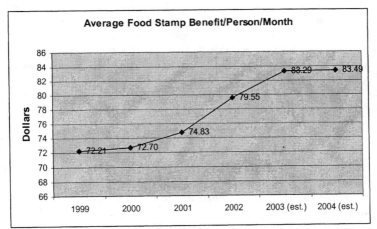

Source: U.S. Department of Agriculture; Available at
http://www.fns.usda.gov/pd/fssummar.htm

WIC

The Special Supplemental Nutrition Program for Women, Infants, and Children (WIC) provides both nutrition education and supplemental foods for pregnant, breastfeeding, and post-partum women, infants, and children. WIC is one of the central components the nations food programs providing assistance to an estimated 7.7 million women and children each month in 2003, up from 7.3 million in 1999, including almost half of all infants born in the United States.[17]

Federal program costs totaled $4.3 billion in fiscal 2002, making WIC the country's third-largest food assistance program in terms of total expenditures.[18] The average monthly benefit per person for WIC recipients ranged from $26.70 in Maine to $44.70 in Hawaii with an average $34.85, only a slight increase over 1999 when it was at $32.52.[19]

In order to reduce costs for providing food supplements to recipients, state WIC agencies engage in cost-saving practices such as negotiating rebate contracts with manufacturers of infant formula; limiting authorized vendors to stores with lower food prices; limiting approved brands, package sizes, forms, or prices; and, negotiating rebates with food manufacturers or suppliers. Advocates and legislators voiced concerns about the possible detrimental effects that price containment practices might have of women and children. A study on the impact of cost containment practices on the nutrition of women, infants and children found that cost-containment practices reduced average food package costs by 0.2 to 21.4 percent, had fewer adverse outcomes for WIC participants.[20]

Child nutrition programs

The National School Lunch Program. In FY 2001, more than 25.4 million children each day got their lunch through the National School Lunch Program.. The National School Lunch Program cost 6.4 billion in FY 2001.[21]

National School Breakfast Program. In FY 2001, this served an average of 7.8 million children every day. That number grew to 8.2 million in FY 2002. For FY 2003, Congress appropriated $1.68 billion for the School Breakfast Program, up from $1.54 billion in Fiscal Year 2002.[22]

The Child and Adult Care Food Program (CACFP). The CACFP provides healthful meals and snacks for children and adults who attend programs that operates in family or group day care homes, child care centers, adult day care centers for elderly and impaired adults, emergency shelters that provide meals to homeless children, and after-school programs that provide educational or enrichment activities.[23] Participation in CACFP has grown 23,000 in 1969 to 2.9 billion in 2002, and has not experienced a decline in participation since 1969 when data began being collected. Federal support for this nutrition program has continued to grow with participation rates (see figure 7.4). In 2002, $1.85 billion was invested in this nutrition program.[24]

Figure 7.4

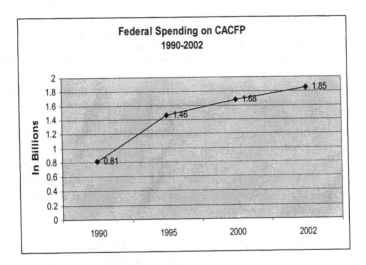

Child Protection and Placement

Child maltreatment

Child protective services (CPS) agencies across the country received 2.7 million referrals representing approximately 5 million children, alleging of child maltreatment in 2001,. Most referrals (56.5%) came from professionals such as teachers, legal and law enforcement personnel, and social service providers. About a third (32.7%) or 870.000 were screened out as not appropriate for CPS and many are referred to more appropriate agencies. The remainder of the referrals were investigated by CPS personnel. Following investigation, the cases were classified into one of the following categories:

- *Substantiate:* allegation of maltreatment or risk of maltreatment was supported by or founded on State law or State policy. This is the most serious classification of a case;
- *Indicated* or *Reason to Suspect:* maltreatment could not be substantiated under State law or policy, but there was reason to suspect that the child might have been maltreated or was at risk of maltreatment;
- *Alternative Response Victim:* the child was identified as a victim when a response other than investigation was provided;
- *Alternative Response Nonvictim:* the child was not victim of maltreatment when a response other than investigation was provided;
- *Unsubstantiated:* no maltreatment occurred or that there was insufficient evidence under State law or policy to conclude that the child was maltreated or was at risk of being maltreated.[25]

More than a quarter of investigations or assessments resulted in a disposition of "Substantiated" (27.5%), "Indicated" (4.4%), or "Alternative Response-Victim" (0.4%). Together, these number indicate that at least one child involved in any such investigation was determined to be a victim. More than half (59.2%) of investigations outcomes were classified as "Unsubstantiated" (see figure 7.5). For each of the past 5 years, the percentage of substantiated reports in any year has not exceeded 29.0 percent, and the percentage of unsubstantiated reports has been less than 60. percent.[26]

Figure 7.5

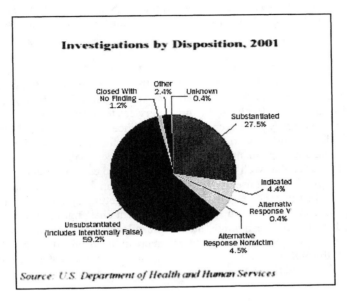

Investigations by Disposition, 2001

Other 2.4%
Unknown 0.4%
Closed With No Finding 1.2%
Substantiated 27.5%
Indicated 4.4%
Alternativ Response V 0.4%
Unsubstantiated (Includes Intentionally False) 59.2%
Alternative Response Nonvictim 4.5%

Source: U.S. Department of Health and Human Services

In 2001, 1,300 children died from child abuse, or slightly less than 2 per 100,000 children. Less than 10 percent (8.8%) of the families in which a child died had received family preservation services in the 5 years prior to the death; and, less than 1 percent (0.9%) of child fatality victims had been reunited with their families following placement prior to their deaths. Deaths that occur while a child is under the custody or supervision of the child welfare agency are especially egregious. Child protective services (CPS) in 48 States reported 18 deaths that occurred in foster care. Approximately 1.5 percent of child fatalities reported by the States occurred in some type of out-of-home placement setting.[27]

President Bush's new initiative, "Promoting Safe and Stable Families," assist states in coordinating services related to child abuse prevention and family preservation, and provides community-based family support, time-limited family reunification and adoption promotion and support services. States are given federal grants to keep children with their biological families, if safe and appropriate, or to place children with adoptive families. The program was funded at $70 million in 2002 and $200 million in 2003. At this point, the program is too new to assess its impact.[28]

To better protect children charged to state child welfare agencies, Congress authorized matching funds for the development of statewide automated childe welfare information systems (SACWIS) and required the Department of Health and Human Services to compile information on children served by state agencies in 1994. Since that time 47 states are either developing or operating a SACWIS, but face many challenges in designing and implementing systems that produce reliable data. State officials agree that such systems are desirable and can contribute to the timeliness of child abuse and neglect investigation, but find that on average the run 21/2 years behind schedule in getting systems up and running. States have faced system development challenges of receiving state funding, and designing systems that reflects their work processes. State also have encountered problems in creating systems that give states' the ability to collect and report reliable adoption, foster care, and child abuse and neglect data.. These barriers include:

- Insufficient caseworker training;
- Inaccurate and incomplete data entry; and,
- Lack of clear and documented guidance on how to report child welfare data

States were mandated to begin reporting data to the Adoption and Foster Care Analysis and Reporting System (AFCARS) in 1995, but few federal reviews of state systems have been conduct to help states in meeting this mandate.[29]

Out of home placements

In 2001, there was an estimated 542,000 children in foster care. Forty-eight percent were in foster family homes (non-relative), 24 percent were in relative foster homes, 18 percent were in group homes or institutions, 4 percent were in pre-adoptive homes, and 6 percent were in other placement types. The distribution of children by type of placement over the four year period from 1998-2001 was unchanged. During FY

2001, 290,000 children entered foster care, and 263,000 children exited foster care. Between 1998 and 2001, entries into foster care stayed relatively stable, while exits increased by 15,000, and the number of children in care at any one point in time dropped by 18,000.[30]

Goals set for children in foster care in 2001 ranged from reunification (44%), to finding an adoptive home (22%), to gaining emancipation (6%). Eight percent of the children were hoping to find a permanent home with a relative or guardian. Eleven percent had not yet established a permanency goal (see figure 7.6). The most notable change in outcome goals set between 1998 and 2001 occurred in the proportion of children who had "No Goal Established." This category decreased by 12 percent.[31]

Figure 7.6

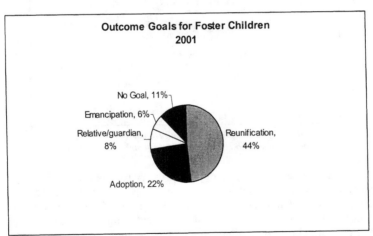

Source: U.S. Department of Health and Human Services

Reunification with family is the most frequent outcome for foster children. Fifty-seven percent of 263,000 children who left foster care in 2001 were reunited with their families. This was down from 62 percent in 1998. Another 18 percent were adopted, 13 percent went to live with a relative or guardian, and 7 percent were emancipated (see figure 7.7). While the number of children reunited with their families decreased by 5 percent from 1998 to 2001, the percentage of children leaving foster care to live with a stable family (reunification, relative, or adoption) actually increase by 6 percent.[32]

Figure 7.7

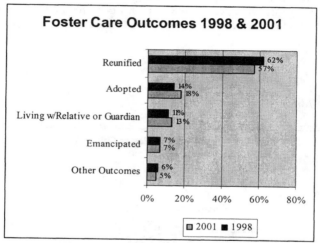

Source: *U.S. Department of Health and Human Services; Available at http://www.calib.com/nccanch/pubs/factsheets/foster.cfm*

Lack of adequate housing is a primary reason for the imminent placement of a family's children or in the delay in reuniting children with their families.[33] The Family Unification Program (FUP) through HUD seeks to address this pressing problem by providing rental subsidies to families with children who have been place or are at risk of placement in foster care primarily because the family lacks adequate housing. FUP helps families' move into more adequate housing through the Housing Choice Voucher Program (section 8). The program was expanded to include foster kids aging out of foster care. They are now eligible for rental assistance for up to 18 months after leaving foster care.[34]

A recent trend reported by states and mental health advocacy organizations is the difficulty that parents are experiencing in accessing mental health services for their children. As a result, parents have been voluntarily placing their children with child welfare agencies or juvenile justice systems in order to get the mental health care that their children need. At the request of the Senate Committee on Governmental Affairs, the GAO conducted a survey of state child welfare directors in all 50 states and the District of Columbia, and county level juvenile justice officials in 17 states with large populations of children. The GAO found that child welfare directors in 19 states and juvenile justice officials in 30 counties estimated that in FY 2001 over 12,700 children were placed into their systems voluntarily by their parents so that their children could receive mental health services. The GAO suggested that this is likely an undercount since many child welfare directors did not have data available, and no state tracks children for these characteristics. The child welfare system is designed for the placement of abused and neglected children only, and the juvenile justice system is designed to place only children who have been delinquent. The GAO reported that these inappropriate placements were influenced by several factors:

- Limitations of both public and private health insurance;
- Inadequate supplies of some mental health services;
- Difficulties accessing services through mental health agencies and schools; and,
- Difficulties meeting eligibility rules for services.[35]

Child Care Assistance

The cost of quality child care has risen so high that it has become prohibitive for many families, and is a barrier for moderate and low-wage earners entering the job market. Urban center-based child care for one 4-year-old child is more than tuition at 4-year public college in most states. Costs range from a high of $8,121 annual in Massachusetts to a low of $3,380 in Mississippi. Table 7.1 compares the cost of child care in the top 10 states with high child care cost with that states cost of tuition for a 4 year public college.[36] For many working families and those wishing to enter the job market, child care assistance is a necessity.

Table 7.1: Cost of Child Care for one 4-Year Old in an Urban Child Care Center

Compared to Cost of College Tuition

State	Cost of Child Care for one 4 Year Old in Urban Child Care Center	Cost of College Tuition in 4-Year Public College
1. Massachusetts	$8121	$4105
2. New York	8060	3983
3. Minnesota	7436	3800
4. Washington	6604	3357
5. New Hampshire	6520	6083
6. Connecticut	6405	4435
7. Rhode Island	6365	4318
8. Iowa	6198	2998
9. Pennsylvania	6188	5610
10. Alaska	6019	2855
11. Wisconsin	6104	3313

Source: Children's Defense Fund; "The State of Children in America's Union: A 2002 Action Guide to Leave No Child Left Behind"

Some studies indicate that after the implementation of TANF in 1997, that access to child care assistance for non-TANF families expanded. A 2002 General Accounting Office (GAO) study found that the numbers of children in non-TANF receiving assistance increased between 10 and 160 percent across states following the 1997 implementation of the 1996 welfare reform law.[37] The majority of states make child care assistance available to TANF families, families transitioning off TANF, and low-income families not associated with TANF. However, in about half of the states not all eligible families who apply for assistance receive it. States often give TANF and transitioning families priority over low-income working families. Since the recession began in 2001, states have had to face difficult budget choices, and some states are beginning to make policy changes that limit access to child care assistance. According to a General Accounting Office (GAO) survey conducted in March-April 2003 to child care administrators in all 50 states and the District of Columbia, since 2001, 35 states gave made key policy changes affecting access to child care assistance. For instance, Nebraska decreased its threshold from 185% or poverty to 120% of poverty in 2002. Likewise New Mexico decreased its eligible threshold in half from 200% of poverty to 100% of poverty. Most of the states (23) have made changes that make child care assistance less available; a few (9) have made policy change that made child care assistance more available, and three states had a mix of changes. Fourteen states reduced availability to child care assistance by lowering the income eligibility threshold. This, in effect, kicks some low-income working families off the child assistance rolls, thus threatening their ability to remain in the work place. As a result of state policy changes, waiting lists for child care assistance are becoming more common. The impact of these policy changes in terms the number of children served is not yet known. Most states are proposing to maintain current funding levels, or decrease child care funding for FY 2004.[38]

Early Childhood Education

The Early Childhood Initiative and Head Start

Every 1$ invested in quality early childhood care and education saves $7 by increasing the likelihood that children will be literate, employed, and enrolled in postsecondary education and less likely to be school dropouts, dependent on welfare, or arrested for criminal activity or delinquency.[39] In April 2002, President Bush announced the Early Childhood Initiative to improve the state of early childhood education, in which too many children come to school unprepared to learn. The initiative includes steps to improve Head Start by direction the Department of Health and Human Services (HHS) to implement a new accountability system to ensure that every Head Start center assesses standards of learning in early literacy, language and numeracy skills. In addition, HHS will implement a national training project with the goal of training all of the nearly 50,000 Head Start teachers this year in the best pre-reading and language teaching techniques for young children. Head Start had modest increases in its budget for 2003 ($6.67 billion) up from $6.54 billion in 2002. The President's budget proposal for 2004 asks for an increase of $148 million. Head Start will serve about 915,000 children in 2003;[40] however, only 3 in 5 eligible children are enrolled in Head Start Programs.[41]

Most states provide some type of state funded pre-kindergarten education for low-income and at risk children, either through Head Start, or other state funded programs. In 2001 Federal head Start enrollments were 804,598 children. Twenty states operate Head Start programs, Twenty-three states operate other state funded pre-kindergarten programs and sixteen states operate Head Start and other state funded pre-kindergarten programs . Eight states offer no state funded pre-kindergarten education (see table 7.2).[42]

Teaching homeless children

The U.S. Department of Education estimates that the number of children and youth who are homeless increased from 841,700 in 1997 to 930,200 in 2000,[43] and the Urban Institute estimates that 1.35 million children will experience homelessness over the course of a year.[44] The McKinney-Vento Act's Education for Homeless Children and Youth program provides financial grant assistance to states and local school districts to implement provisions guaranteeing school access and stability. Congress appropriated $55 million for this program in FY 2003. Fifteen million dollars less than the $70 million Congress authorized. The recently reauthorized McKinney-Vento Act requires school districts to stabilized children in their original schools, including providing transportation so they can continue their education without disruption; it also requires that children experiencing homelessness be immediately enrolled in school if they are moving to a new school.[45]

Table 7.2: Funded Early Childhood Education Programs by State

Offer Head Start Education Only	Offer Other State Funded Pre-Kindergarten Education Only	Offer Head Start & Other State Funded Pre-Kindergarten Education	Offer no State Funded Pre-Kindergarten Education
Alaska	Alabama	Connecticut	Idaho
Delaware	Arizona	District of Columbia	Indiana
New Hampshire	Arkansas	Florida	Mississippi
Oregon	California	Hawaii	Montana
	Colorado	Kansas	North Dakota
	Georgia	Maine	South Dakota
	Illinois	Massachusetts	Utah
	Iowa	Minnesota	Wyoming
	Kentucky	New Jersey	
	Louisiana	New Mexico	
	Maryland	New York	
	Michigan	Ohio	
	Missouri	Oklahoma	
	Nebraska	Rhode Island	
	Nevada	Washington	
	North Carolina	Wisconsin	
	Pennsylvania		
	South Carolina		
	Tennessee		
	Texas		
	Vermont		
	Virginia		
	West Virginia		
TOTAL: 4	23	16	8

Source: Children's Defense Fund; "The State of Children in America's Union: A 2002 Action Guide to Leave No Child Left Behind"

ENDNOTES

1. Children's Defense Fund, *Child Care Advocacy Network Newsletters,* (Washington DC: September 5, 2003). Available at http://www.childrensdefense.org/childcare/newsletters/2003_090 5.php Accessed September 25, 2003

2. National Center for Children in Poverty, "Low-Income Children in the United States, 2003," Columbia University Mailman School of Public Health, New York, NY. Available at http://www.nccp.org/pub_cpf03.html Accessed September 9, 2003.

3. Children's Defense Fund, *The State of Children in America's Union: A 2002 Action Guide to Leave No Child Left Behind,* Washington DC. Available at http://www.childrensdefense.org/pdf/cc_statedev01.pdf Accessed September 23, 2003.

4. Ibid.

5. Annual Demographic Survey: March Supplement, Table HI01, *Health Insurance Coverage Status and Type of Coverage by Selected Characteristics: 2001,* A Joint Project between the Bureau of Labor Statistics and the Bureau of the Census, (Washington DC: September 30, 2002). Available at http://ferret.bls.census.gov/macro/032002/health/h01_001.htm Accessed September 27, 2003.

6. Children's Defense Fund, *CHIP & Medicaid FAQ,* Washington DC. Available at http://www.childrensdefense.org/hs_faqs.php Accessed September 25, 2003.

7. Centers for Medicaid and Medicare Services, State Children's Health Insurance Program, *Fiscal Year 2002 Number of Children Ever Enrolled in SCHIP—Preliminary Data Summary,* (Washington DC: January 30, 2003). Available at http://cms.hhs.gov/schip/schip02.pdf Accessed September 27, 2003.

8. Centers for Medicaid and Medicare Services, State Children's Health Insurance Program, *Aggregate Enrollment Statistics for the 50 States and the District of Columbia for Federal Fiscal Year (FFY) 2000,* Washington DC. Available at http://cms.hhs.gov/schip/fy2000.pdf Accessed September 27, 2003

9. U.S. Department of Health and Human Services, Office of Budget, *President's Budget for HHS, 2000, 2001, 2002, 2003, 2004,* Washington DC. Available at http://www.hhs.gov/budget/docbudget.htm Accessed September 27, 2003.

10. Linda Weinreb, Cheryl Wehler, Jennifer Perloff, Richard Scott, David Hosmer, Linda Sabor, and Craig Gundesen, "Hunger: Its Impact on Children's Health and Mental Health," *Pediatrics,* Vol. 110, No. 4 (Elk Grove Village, IL: American Academy of Pediatrics) October, 2002.

11. Mark Nord and Margaret Andrews "Putting Food on the Table: Household Food Security in the United States," *Amber Waves: The Economics of Food, Farming, Natural Resources and Rural America, (*Washington DC: U.S. Department of Agriculture) February, 2003. Available at http://www.ers.usda.gov/AmberWaves/Feb03/Features/PuttingFood.htm Accessed September 27, 2003.

12. U.S. Department of Agriculture, *Food Stamp Program Participation and Costs,* (Washington DC: August 26, 2003). Available at http://www.fns.usda.gov/pd/fssummar.htm Accessed September 27, 2003.

13. Mark Nord and Margaret Andrews "Putting Food on the Table: Household Food Security in the United States," *Amber Waves: The Economics of Food, Farming, Natural Resources and Rural America, (*Washington DC: U.S. Department of Agriculture) February, 2003. Available at http://www.ers.usda.gov/AmberWaves/Feb03/Features/PuttingFood.htm Accessed September 27, 2003.

14. Bernadette D. Proctor and Joseph Dalaker, "Poverty in the United States, 2001" *Current Population Reports: Consumer Income,* (Washington DC: U.S. Census Bureau) September, 2002.

15. Office of Analysis, Nutrition, and Evaluation, *Characteristics of Food Stamp Households: Fiscal Year 2002,* (Washington DC: U.S. Department of Agriculture) July, 2003.

16. U.S. Department of Agriculture, *Food Stamp Program: Average Monthly Benefit per Persons,* (Washington DC: August 26, 2003). Available at http://www.fns.usda.gov/pd/fsavgben.htm Accessed September 27, 2003.

17. U.S. Department of Agriculture, *WIC Program Participation and Costs,* August 26, 2003.Available at http://www.fns.usda.gov/pd/wisummary.htm Accessed September 27, 2003.

18. Briefing Room: The WIC Program *Economic Research Services,* (Washington DC: U.S. Department of Agriculture March 10, 2003. Available at http://www.ers.usda.gov/Briefing/WIC/ Accessed September 27, 2003.

19. U.S. Department of Agriculture, *WIC Program: Average Monthly Benefit per Person,* August 28, 2003.Available at http://www.fns.usda.gov/pd/wifavgfd$.htm

20. John A. Kirlin, Nancy Cole, and Christopher Logan, Assessment of WIC Cost-Containment Practices: Final Report, *Economic Research Services, E-FAN No. (03-005)* 342 pp, (Washington DC: U.S. Department of Agriculture0 February 2003. Available at http://www.ers.usda.gov/publications/efan03005/ Accessed September 27, 2003.

21. U.S. Department of Health and Family Services, *National School Lunch Program http://www.fns.usda.gov/cnd/Lunch/AboutLunch/AboutNLS P.htm* Accessed September 22, 2003.

22. U.S. Department of Health and Family Services, *National School Breakfast Program* http://www.fns.usda.gov/cnd/Breakfast/AboutBFast/bfastfacts.ht m Accessed September 22, 2003.

23. *The Nation Nutrition Safety Net,* U.S. Department of Agriculture (Washington DC: April 3, 2003). Available at http://www.fns.usda.gov/fsec/toolkit/CACFP.htm Accessed September 27, 2003.

24. *Child and Adult Care Food Program,* U.S. Department of Agriculture (Washington DC: August 28, 2003) Available at http://www.fns.usda.gov/pd/ccsummar.htm Accessed September 27, 2003.

25. U.S. Department of Health and Human Services, *Child Maltreatment, 2001,* (Washington DC: 2001) Available at http://www.acf.hhs.gov/programs/cb/publications/cm01/outcover .htm Accessed September 26, 2003

26. Ibid.

27. Ibid.
28. U.S. Department of Health and Human Services, *HHS Invests In America's Children,* (Washington DC: April 11, 2002). Available at http://www.hhs.gov/news/press/2002pres/children.html Accessed September 27, 2003.
29. U.S. General Accounting Office, Report to Congressional Requesters, *Child Welfare: Most States are Developing Statewide Information Systems, but the Reliability of Child Welfare Data could be Improved,* (Washington DC: July, 2003). Available at www.gao.gov/cgi-bin/getrpt?GAO-03-809 Accessed September 7, 2003.
30. National Clearing House on Child Abuse and Neglect Information, *Foster Care National Statistics,* (Washington DC: U.S. Department of Health and Human Services). June, 2003.
31. Ibid.
32. Ibid.
33. Child Welfare League of America, *Family Reunification Program Information,* Washington DC, 2000. Available at www.swla.org/programs/housing Accessed September 10, 2003.
34. Child Welfare League of America, *Housing and Homelessness: Housing Solutions for Child Welfare Families,* Washington DC. Available at http://www.cwla.org/programs/housing/ Accessed September 10, 2003.
35. U.S. General Accounting Office, Testimony before the U.S. Senate Committee on Governmental Affairs, *Child Welfare and Juvenile Justice: Several Factors Influence the Placement of Children Solely to Obtain Mental Health Services* (Washington DC: July 17, 2003). Available at http://www.gao.gov/new.items/d03865t.pdf Accessed September 26, 2003.
36. Children's Defense Fund, *The State of Children in America's Union: A 2002 Action Guide to Leave No Child Left Behind,* Washington DC. Available at http://www.childrensdefense.org/pdf/cc_statedev01.pdf Accessed September 23, 2003.
37. U.S. General Accounting Office, *Welfare Reform: States Provide TANF-Funded Work Support Services to Many Low-Income*

Families who do not Receive Cash Assistance, GAO-02-615, (Washington, DC: April 10, 2002).

38. General Account Office, "Recent State Policy Changes Affecting the Availability of Child Care Assistance," *Briefing for Staff of Rep. Benjamin Cardin Ranking Minority Member Subcommittee on Human Resources Committee on Ways and Means House of Representatives,* (Washington DC: April, 24, 2003).

39. Children's Defense Fund, *The State of Children in America's Union: A 2002 Action Guide to Leave No Child Left Behind,* Washington DC. Available at http://www.childrensdefense.org/pdf/cc_statedev01.pdf Accessed September 23, 2003.

40. U.S. Department of Health and Human Services, *HHS Invests In America's Children,* (Washington DC: April 11, 2002). Available at http://www.hhs.gov/news/press/2002pres/children.html Accessed September 27, 2003.

41. Children's Defense Fund, *The State of Children in America's Union: A 2002 Action Guide to Leave No Child Left Behind,* Washington DC. Available at http://www.childrensdefense.org/pdf/cc_statedev01.pdf Accessed September 23, 2003.

42. Ibid.

43. U.S. Department of Education, as cited in *People Need Education,* National Coalition for the Homeless, Washington DC, 2002. Available at www.nationalhomeless.org/facts/education.html Accessed September 10, 2003.

44. Urban Institute as cited in *People Need Education,* National Coalition for the Homeless, Washington DC, 2002. Available at www.nationalhomeless.org/facts/education.html Accessed September 10, 2003.

45. National Coalition for the Homeless, *People Need Education,* Washington DC 2002. Available at www.nationalhomeless.org/facts/education.html Accessed September 10, 2003.

SECTION EIGHT

CARING FOR THE ELDERLY

Social Security Old-Age and Survivors Insurance

Following the stock market bubble burst, many people planning to retire in the near future, postponed their retirement plans, and some who had already retired reentered the labor market because of losses in the stock market. Social Security has become even more important as a stable component of the retirement portfolio for those 55 and order. A recent study of over 2000 pre-retirees conducted by the American Association of Retire Persons (AARP) found that, for most respondents, their personal definition of retirement included some form of work. Those who expected to work in retirement were considering a variety of occupations, including positions related to teaching, office support, crafts, retail sales, and health care. The top three reasons give for working in retirement by those planning to do so (this included 1020 respondents) were

- Need the money;
- Need health care benefits;
- To stay mentally active.[1]

The pay-as-you-go system: Collection and distribution of funds

Social Security benefits paid out to beneficiaries each year are primarily funded through payroll taxes, and most of the payroll taxes collected from today's workers are used to pay benefits to today's recipients (a pay-as-you-go system). In 2002, 85 percent of the Old-Age and Survivors Insurance and Disability Insurance Trust Fund (OASIDI) receipts came from payroll taxes (see figure 8.1). The remainder came from income taxes on Social Security benefits (2%), and interest earned on the government bonds held by the trust funds (13%). In all, $627 billion in revenues were collected in 2002. Seventy-three percent of the revenues were used to pay out benefits, 1 percent was used to administer the OASIDI programs, and 26 percent remained in OASIDI trust fund to bear interests to be used to pay future beneficiaries (see figure 8.1).[2]

Each year, OASIDI beneficiaries receive an increase in benefits based on the Consumer Price Index, or inflation from the previous year. This cost-of-living (COLA) was 3.5% in 2001[3] and 1.4% for 2003 (see table 8.1).[4] To ensure that OASIDI recipients receive their full COLA, Congress passed the Consolidated Appropriation Act, 2001 that requires that payments to beneficiaries be made to compensate for any shortfall resulting from a technical error in the computation of the Consumer Price Index.[5]

Figure 8.1: Sources and Uses of Social Security Revenues in 2002

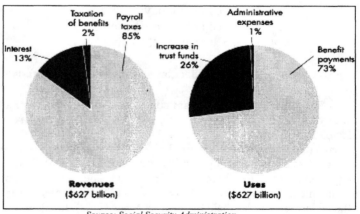

Source: Social Security Administration

Table 8.1: Cost-of-Living Adjustments for OASDI Recipients

YEAR	COLA (%)
2001	3.5%
2002	2.6
2003	**1.4**

Source: Social Security Administration

The average worker's wage taxed for OASIDI payroll taxes was $34,731 in 2003 (estimate) up from $32,922 in 2001. The maximum earnings subject to payroll taxes in 2003 was $87,000,[6] up from $80,400 in 2001 and $84,900 in 2002.[7] In 2003, $890 in earnings equaled one quarter of coverage or one credit. The maximum earnings needed for four credits or a full year of coverage in 2003 was $3,560. It is estimated that the average earner will pay $1841 in payroll taxes in 2003.[8]

Historically, retirees were limited to the amount of money they could earn without penalty as an OASI recipient. The Senior Citizens' Freedom to Work Act of 2000 eliminated the Social Security retirement earnings test.[9] Recipients receiving partial benefits before attaining full retirement age will continue to have one dollar withheld from their benefits for every two dollars earned above the annual limit of $11,520 until attaining full retirement age. During the year that full retirement age is attained, beneficiaries will have one dollar of benefits withheld for every 3 dollars earned above the annual limit, which increases substantially to $30,720.[10] In the calendar year after full retirement age is attained, no penalty is applied, and the retiree is free to earn as much income as they like or are able (see table 8.2).[11]

Table 8.2: Retirement Earnings Test 2003 (In dollars)

Period	Annually	Monthly
Ages 62-64 ($1 for $2 withholding rate)	$11,520	$ 960
Calendar year attaining retirement age ($1 for $3 withholding rate) [a]	30,720	2,560
After calendar year attaining retirement age or older	No limit	No limit
a. Test no longer applies beginning in the month in which retirement age is reached.		

Source: Social Security Administration

Who relies on Social Security?

In 2001, 91% of married couples and non-married persons aged 65 or older received Social Security benefits. Most people rely on social security in their retirement years. For most people, social security income makes up 50 percent or more of their income (see figure 8.2). For a third of retirees, social security income constitutes 90 percent of their income, and for 20 percent it is their only source of income (see figure 8.2).[12]

Figure 8.2: Percentage of the Aged Receiving Social Security by Relative Importance of Benefits to Total Income

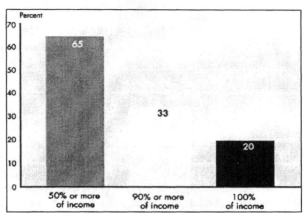

Source: Social Security Administration

How many people receive Social Security benefits?

In 2002, more than 46 million people were receiving Social Security benefits. Most (63%) were retired workers, 12 percent were disabled workers, and 25 percent were spouses, children, survivors, or dependents of retired or disabled workers (see figure 8.3).[13]

Figure 8.3: Beneficiaries, by Type

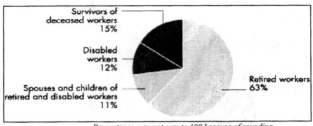

Percentages may not sum to 100 because of rounding
Source: Social Security Administration

Estimated benefit amounts for 2003

The two factors that most impact the amount a retired worker will receive in social security benefits are: 1) the average wages earned during their work life, and 2) the age of retirement. The higher the average earnings during a working career, the higher the retirement benefit will be. An individual's retirement benefit is also affected by the age at which they retire. Those choosing early retirement at age 62 (the earliest age possible to receive retirement benefits) will receive a percentage of the full benefit that they would have received if they had waited to retire at their full retirement age. The full benefit retirement age is slowly escalating to 67, and is dependent on the year you in which you were born (see table 8.3). For those born 1943-1954, full retirement age is 66. This age requirement will increase by 2 months a year until age 67 is required for full benefits for those born in 1960 or later. If your full retirement age is 65 and you choose to collect social security benefits at 62, you will receive approximately 80% of your benefits; however, if your full retirement age is 67 and you retire at 62, you will only receive about 70 percent of your full benefits. Generally, early retirement will give you about the same total benefit over your life time; it will just be paid in smaller amounts over a longer period of time. Those who choose to delay retirement beyond their full retirement age are entitled to an increase in retirement benefits. The size of the increase is dependent upon the year in which you were born, ranging from a 3% increase for those born 1917-1924, to an 8% increase for those born in 1943 or later.[14]

Table 8.4 show the differences in retirement benefits based on average lifetime wages, and age at retirement. A worker who had worked continuously at low wages (45% of the national average wage) and who claimed benefits at age 62 in January 2003 would receive a monthly benefit of $572. If that same worker delayed retirement to age 70, her/his benefit would increase to $833. A high income earner would receive a benefit of $1236 when retiring at age 62, and increase that benefit to $1786 if they waited to retire at age 70. The maximum retirement benefit possible in 2003 was $2045.[15]

Table 8.3: Age to Receive Full Social Security Benefits

Year of Birth	Full Retirement Age
1937 or earlier	65
1938	65 and 2 months
1939	65 and 4 months
1940	65 and 6 months
1941	65 and 8 months
1942	65 and 10 months
1943-1954	66
1955	66 and 2 months
1956	66 and 4 months
1957	66 and 6 months
1958	66 and 8 months
1959	66 and 10 months
1960 and later	67

Source: Social Security Administration

143

Table 8.4: Estimated Benefits by Income Level and Retirement Age (2003)

Hypothetical benefit (in dollars)			
Earnings	Age 62	Age 65	Age 70
Low	572	701	833
Average	943	1,158	1,387
High	1,236	1,513	1,786
Maximum	1,404	1,721	2,045

SOURCE: Social Security Administration, Office of the Chief Actuary.
NOTE: Low earnings are defined as 45% of the national average index, average earnings are equal to the index, high earnings are 160% of the index, and maximum earnings are equal to the OASDI contribution and benefits base.

Source: Social Security Administration

How sustainable is Social Security?

As noted earlier, the total social security benefits paid out in 2002 were 73 percent of the receipts, or $454 billion. The income to the OASIDI Trust Fund was $627 billion. OASIDI income is expected to outpace outlays until 2010.[16] The number of retired workers is projected to grow rapidly beginning in 2008, when the post-World War II baby boomers (those born 1946-1965) begin to reach early retirement age. There are approximately 80 million baby boomers, and the number of retirees is projected to double in less than 30 years. To compound this stress on the Social Security Trust Fund, life expectancy is increasing while the birth rate is low. As a result, the ratio of workers paying Social Security taxes to people collecting benefits will fall from 3.3 to 1 today to 2.1 to 1 by 2031 (see figure 8.4). There will not be enough workers to pay scheduled retiree benefits at current tax rates.[17]

144

Figure 8.4: Ratio of Workers to Social Security Beneficiaries

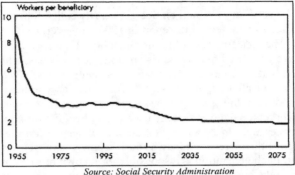

Source: Social Security Administration

The surplus of trust funds will diminish as the baby boomers continue to retire from 2011-2040, and age. The trust fund balance is projected to start to decline in 2026.[18] At present rates of benefit payout and payroll tax collection, the trust fund is projected to be exhausted by 2042. In present-value terms, the shortfall over the next 75 years is $3.5 trillion, which is roughly equal to the total U.S. government debt held by the public today (see figure 8.5).[19]

Figure 8.5: Cumulative Income less Cost Based on Present Taxes and Scheduled Benefits

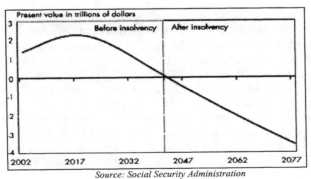

Source: Social Security Administration

The Advisory Council on Social Security called for reforms to the social security system in its report in 1996, however, Congress has yet to act. The concerns about the sustainability of the social security system have generated much discussion among economists, who agree that the tax burden necessary to sustain the system beyond 2042 is prohibitive. One alternative is to switch from a pay-as-you-to system to a prefunded system. In the current pay-as-you-go system, one generation (current workers) pay taxes that are used to pay benefits for another (retired) generation. In a prefunded system, each generation funds its own retirement by investing today's social security taxes for tomorrow's retirement. Each generation is responsible for its own retirement rather than placing the burden on the next generation. Using this system, the fund never runs out of money. To switch to a prefunded system, whether public or private, would require a one time transition cost to current generations of $10 trillion. While this is probably politically difficult to sell, it could be phased in over time to ease the burden. What is equally politically unpalatable is the needed increase in taxes and/or decrease in benefits required to sustain the current system beyond 2042.[20] Whatever approach is selected to address the ever-looming problem of sustainability of the current system, economist, advocates, and legislators all agree that the time to act is now.

Ensuring the Health of the Elderly through Medicare

Medicare has provided health security for older Americans for more than 30 years. The number of older Americans who are covered by Medicare has grown dramatically since its implementation, and is expected to expand even more in the years to come as the baby-boomers move into retirement age. In 2000, 31.1 million elderly Americans were receiving Medicare benefits, and that number is expected to double by 2030 (see figure 8.6).[21] With the rise in the number of enrollees in Medicare, the federal government has made greater economic commitments to the health and well-being of older Americans. In 1970, federal expenditures for Medicare were $7.1 billion. In 2002 the amount was $256.8 billion. That amount is expected to grow to $388.2 by 2008 (see figure 8.7).[22]

Figure 8.6: Number of Medicare Beneficiaries 1970-2030

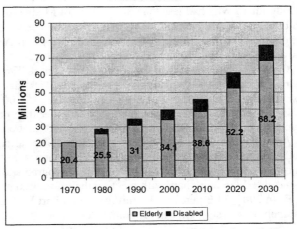

Source: Centers for Medicare and Medicaid; Available at http://cms.hhs.gov/charts/default.asp

Figure 8.7

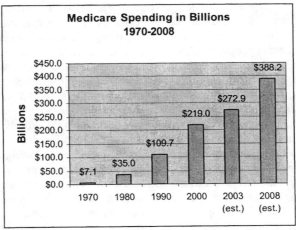

Source: Budget of the United States FY 2004 Historical Tables

In 2003, most people enrolled in Medicare Hospital Insurance (HI) did not pay a monthly premium. For those retired workers who had 40 quarters of Medicare covered employment, there was no premium. For individuals who had less than 30 quarters of Medicare covered employment, monthly premiums were $316, and those with 30-39 quarters paid premiums of $174. The deductible for Part A in 2003 was $840 and co-insurance for hospital stays was $210 a day for the 61st to the 90th day of hospitalization for each benefit period. The co-insurance amount increased to $420 a day for the 91st to the 150th day. Skilled nursing home co-insurance was $105 a day for the 21st-100th day of care. Part B of Medicare which covers medical care other than hospital care is supported in part by participant premiums. In 2003, that premium was $58.70 per month. The deductible for part B was $100 after which enrollees paid 20% of the Medicare approved amount for services.[23] Some states have established Medicare Buy-in programs to help low-income elderly to help them with meeting their premium payments of part B. In 2001, 11.3 percent (3.7 million) of all Part B elderly enrollees were members in state Buy-in programs.[24]

The High Cost of Prescription Drugs

While it is widely acknowledged by conservatives and liberals alike that Medicare has been instrumental in improving the health and quality of live for older Americans, many of the costly medical needs of most older people (such as eyeglasses, hearing aids, and prescription drugs) are not covered by Medicare insurance. For older Americans, the greatest out of pocket medical expense is for prescription drugs. And, as the growth of health care costs (including drugs) has outpaced inflation by nearly 300 percent each year over the past decade, the cost of prescription drugs is requiring large portions of the elderly's income. For the low income elderly, the cost of prescription drugs has become prohibitive, and many have sought avenues for purchasing drugs at affordable prices through using generic drugs, and through the re-importation of drugs from Canada. Seniors can order their prescription drugs from Canada at a fraction of what they would pay for them in the U.S. The Federal Drug Administration has voiced concerns about this practice since Canadian drugs have not been FDA approved and therefore drug safety cannot be guaranteed. Drug companies are crying

'foul play' because other countries are able to manufacture and sell prescription drugs at much lower costs than U.S manufacturers who have had to
incur the cost of research and development of the very drugs for which foreign competitors are underselling them.

State governors have put pressure on Congress to do something about adopting a plan to help the six million poor elderly pay for their costly prescription drugs. State governors have been specifically concerned about this 'dually eligible' population. The 'dually eligible', are the poor elderly who are eligible for both Medicare and Medicaid. In June 2003, both the House and the Senate passed different versions of legislation to add prescription drug coverage to the Medicare program. Both bills remain in Conference Committee where legislators are trying to work out their differences.[25] Both bills include 1) a budget limit of $400 billion over 10 years; 2) income protection; 3) a high catastrophic cap; 4) use privatization through health insurers and drug companies to deliver the benefits; and, 4) a gap in coverage. The Senate bill would be implemented in 2006 and includes a $35 monthly premium and $275 deductible.[26] The House bill also has a $35 premium, but penalizes older Americans by making it more expensive for those who wish to stay in the traditional Medicare program. The American Association of Retired Persons (AARP) opposes both bills as they stand and is advocating for the following changes in the final bill when it emerged from the Conference Committee:

- New Premium Structure—the House bill creates a competitive structure that threatens to destabilized Medicare and raise premiums in future years for those who want to stay in the traditional Medicare program;
- Access and Stability of the Drug Benefit---Create a Federal Fallback Plan—The House bill does not guarantee that a stable drug benefit will be available in all parts of the country;
- "Means-Testing" the Benefit—The house bill would vary the level of catastrophic cap based on income. AARP feels that all Medicare beneficiaries need to have access to the same level of protection;
- Dual Eligible Beneficiaries—The Senate bill does not guarantee the Medicare drug benefit to seniors who are also eligible for the

low-income Medicaid program. AARP supports the notion that all Medicare beneficiaries should receive the drug benefit through Medicare to protect the social insurance status of Medicare.[27]

The Senate version of the prescription drug legislation excluded the 'dually eligible' population, outraging governors. States are not required to cover prescription drugs under Medicaid, but all states do. States spend about $40 billion a year on 'dually eligible' older citizens. About $7 billion of that is for prescription drugs. The Kaiser Commission on Medicaid and the Uninsured estimated that states could spend $100 billion over the next ten years for prescription drugs for the elderly[28]. The House bill slowly phases out state financial responsibility for prescription drugs over a 15-year period. Both bills contain provisions for the re-importation of prescription drugs. The National Governors' Association has shown unanimous support for the House bill because of its dual eligible coverage;[29] however, others are concerned that the House version would undermine the spirit of Medicare and migrate the program to a means-tested program.

The High Cost of Nursing Home Care through Medicaid

Medicaid is the single larges public source of funding for long-term care, and has increasingly become a large portion of state and federal budgets.[30] The federal outlays for Medicaid have grown dramatically over the past 20+ years as the cost of health care inflation has consistently outpaced the inflation rates. In 1980 the federal outlay for Medicaid was $14 billion. In 2003, it is estimated to be $162.5 billion (see figure 8.8).[31]

Figure 8.8

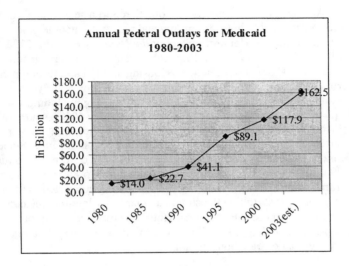

As part of the Omnibus Reconciliation Act of 1980, the Boren Amendment required states to reimburse nursing facilities at rates that were reasonable and adequate to meet the cost incurred by efficiently and economically operated nursing facilities. The Balanced Budge Act of 1997 repealed the Boren Amendment. Since then, states have implemented payment policies that constrain Medicaid expenditures, which some contend have undermined the quality of care provided for Medicaid recipients.[32] With the erosion of the tax base for most states as a result of the recession, Medicaid is consuming larger portions of state budgets, and states are considering cutbacks in the program. President Bush's federal budget requests for fiscal year 2004 proposed a reworking of Medicaid between the federal government and the states, however, details have not yet been spelled out. One approach mentioned by the administration is the conversion of Medicaid to a block grant fund to the states.[33] Many states used the Reed Redistribution Funds appropriated through the unemployment trust fund to meet Medicaid shortfalls (see section five).[34]

Housing Assistance for the Elderly

Advocates for the elderly and others report a severe shortage of suitable and affordable housing for low and moderate-income older persons. According to Harvard's *State of the Nation's Housing 2002*,[35] 8.4 million of the nation's 21 million elderly households have incomes less than $10,500 annually. The U.S. Housing and Urban Development Department (HUD)[36] reports that more than 7.4 million elderly households pay more than they can afford for housing, including 1.4 million very low income elderly households who pay 50% or more of their income for housing. Some live in substandard housing, and none of the households mentioned here received any housing assistance. Since 1993, the HUD elderly housing budget has diminished from $1.1 billion to $779 million in FY 2002. This will construct only 5,800 units. At the same time, some affordable housing units are being converted to market-rate housing, thus shrinking the supply available for low-income elderly households even more. The National Housing Trust[37] reported that 82,897 primarily elderly federally-assisted units are at risk of being converted to market-rate housing units.

HUD officials agree that the most pressing housing problem for the elderly is affordability. Approximately 3.3 million elderly households are very low income. The Section 202 Supportive Housing for the Elderly Program provides capital grants to nonprofit organizations to develop affordable rental housing for the elderly. Unfortunately, Section 202 program assist only about 8% of the low-income elderly or about 260,000 households nationwide. Section 202 not only ensures that residents receive rental assistance, but also access to services that promote independent living. Problems in completing development projects for Section 202 housing have been linked to slow pay by HUD, and insufficient grant funds to develop the housing projects[38].

ENDNOTES

1. American Association of Retired Persons, *Staying Ahead of the Curve 2003: The AARP Working in Retirement Study* (Washington DC: September, 2003). Available at

http://research.aarp.org/econ/multiwork_2003.html Accessed September 28, 2003.

2. Social Security Administration, *Fast Facts & Figures about Social Security*, Washington DC, 2003. http://www.ssa.gov/policy/docs/chartbooks/fast_facts/2003/ff2003.html#financing Accessed September 13, 2003

3. Social Security Administration, *The fiscal year 2003 budget,* Washington DC.

4. Social Security Administration, *Fast Facts & Figures about Social Security*, Washington DC, 2003. http://www.ssa.gov/policy/docs/chartbooks/fast_facts/2003/ff2003.html#financing Accessed September 13, 2003

5. Social Security Administration, *2001 OASDI Trustee's Report,* Washington DC.

6. Social Security Administration, *Fast Facts & Figures about Social Security*, Washington DC, 2003. http://www.ssa.gov/policy/docs/chartbooks/fast_facts/2003/ff2003.html#financing Accessed September 13, 2003

7. Social Security Administration, *The fiscal year 2003 budget,* Washington DC.

8. Social Security Administration, *Fast Facts & Figures about Social Security*, Washington DC, 2003. http://www.ssa.gov/policy/docs/chartbooks/fast_facts/2003/ff2003.html#financing Accessed September 13, 2003.

9. Social Security Administration, *2001 OASDI Trustee's Report,* Washington DC.

10. Social Security Administration, *Social Security Retirement Benefits,* Washington DC, 2003.

11. Social Security Administration, *Fast Facts & Figures about Social Security*, Washington DC, 2003. http://www.ssa.gov/policy/docs/chartbooks/fast_facts/2003/ff2003.html#financing Accessed September 13, 2003

12. Ibid.

13. Ibid.

14. Social Security Administration, *Social Security Retirement Benefits,* Washington DC, 2003.

15. Social Security Administration, *Fast Facts & Figures about Social Security*, Washington DC, 2003.

http://www.ssa.gov/policy/docs/chartbooks/fast_facts/2003/ff200
3.html#financing   Accessed September 13, 2003

16. Social Security Administration, *3001 OASDI Trustee's Report,* Washington DC.

17. Social Security Administration, *Fast Facts & Figures about Social Security,* Washington DC, 2003.
http://www.ssa.gov/policy/docs/chartbooks/fast_facts/2003/ff200
3.html#financing   Accessed September 13, 2003

18. Alan D. Viard, "Pay-as-you-go Social Security and the Aging of America: An Economic Analysis," *Economic and Financial Policy Review,* Dallas: Federal Reserve Bank of Dallas, Vol. 1, No. 4, p. 9.

19. Social Security Administration, *Fast Facts & Figures about Social Security,* Washington DC, 2003.
http://www.ssa.gov/policy/docs/chartbooks/fast_facts/2003/ff200
3.html#financing   Accessed September 13, 2003

20. Alan D. Viard, "Pay-as-you-go Social Security and the Aging of America: An Economic Analysis," *Economic and Financial Policy Review,* Dallas: Federal Reserve Bank of Dallas, Vol. 1, No. 4, pp.6-8.

21. Center for Medicare and Medicaid, *CMS Facts and Figures,* Washington DC. Available at
http://cms.hhs.gov/charts/default.asp Accessed September 28, 2003.

22. Budget of the United States, Fiscal Year 2004, *Historical Tables,* Online via GPO Access [wais.acess.gop.gov]. Accessed September 11, 2003.

23. Centers for Medicare and Medicaid, *Medicare Premium Amounts for 2003,* Washington DC. Available at
http://www.medicare.gov/Basics/Amounts2003.asp
Accessed September 28, 2003.

24. Centers for Medicare and Medicaid, *Medicare State Buy-in for SMI 1998-2001,* (Washington DC: September, 2002). Available at
http://www.cms.hhs.gov/researchers/pubs/datacompendium/200
2/02pg33.pdf Accessed September 28, 2003.

25. THOMAS, *Legislative Information on the Internet,* Available at
www.thomas.loc.gov Accessed September 28, 2003.

26. American Association of Retired Persons, *What's happening in Congress on a Medicare Prescription Drug Benefit?* (Washington DC: May 13, 2003). Available at www.aarp.org/Articles/a2003-05-13-medrxstatus/tools/printable Accessed September 28, 2003.

27. Ibid.

28. Kaiser Commission on Medicaid and the Uninsured as cited in Erin Madigan, *U.S. House Medicare Plan Backed by Govs Conference,* Stateline.org, August 17, 2003. Available at http://www.stateline.org/story.do?storyId=320914 Accessed August 28, 2003.

29. Erin Madigan, *U.S. House Medicare Plan Backed by Govs Conference,* Stateline.org, August 17, 2003. Available at http://www.stateline.org/story.do?storyId=320914 Accessed August 28, 2003.

30. American Association for Homes and Services for the Aging, *Medicaid: Paying for Nursing Home Care,* Washington DC May, 2003 Available at www.aahsa.org Accessed September 9, 2003.

31. Budget of the United States, Fiscal Year 2004, *Historical Tables,* Online via GPO Access [wais.acess.gop.gov]. Accessed September 11, 2003.

32. American Association for Homes and Services for the Aging, *Medicaid: Paying for Nursing Home Care,* Washington DC May, 2003 Available at www.aahsa.org Accessed September 9, 2003.

33. Ibid.

34. General Accounting Office, *States' use of the 2002 Reed Act Distribution,* Briefing GOA-03-496, Washington DC, February 24, 2003.

35. *State of the Nation's Housing 2002,* Harvard University, as cited in American Association of Homes and Services for the Aging, *Affordable Elderly Housing: The HUD FY 2004 Budget,*(Washington DC: 2003).

36. U.S. Department of Urban and Housing Development, as cited in American Association of Homes and Services for the Aging, *Affordable Elderly Housing: The HUD FY 2004 Budget,*(Washington DC: 2003).

37. National Housing Trust, as cited in American Association of Homes and Services for the Aging, *Affordable Elderly Housing: The HUD FY 2004 Budget,*(Washington DC: 2003).
38. U.S. General Accounting Office, Report to the Committee on Aging, U.S. Senate, *Elderly Housing: Project Funding and other Factors Delay Assistance to Needy Households,* (Washington DC: May, 2003) Available at www.gao.gov/cgi-bin/getrpt?GAO-03-512. Accessed August 26, 2003.]

SECTION NINE

CARING FOR THE DISABLED

Who are the Disabled?

During the Census 2000, 49.7 million people with some type of long lasting condition or disability were identified. They represented 19.3 percent of the 257.2 million people who were aged 5 and older in the civilian noninstitutionalized population. This represented nearly one person in five. Non-white populations were more likely to suffer from disabilities (see table 9.1). Blacks and Native Americans experience the highest disability rates at 24.3% each and Asians had the lowest rate at 16.6%.[1]

Table 9.1: Disability Rate by Race
2000

Race	Disability Rate
White	18.5%
Black	24.3%
Native American	24.3%
Asian	16.6%
Hawaiian/Pacific Islander	19.0%
Hispanic/Latino	20.9%
Multiracial	19.9%

Source: U.S. Census Bureau

Providing a Measure of Income Security

For many disabled people, Disability Insurance (DI) under OASDI and/or Supplement Security Income (SSI) is an important part of their income security. Only a small portion of disabled persons qualify for DI. Workers who have met the requirement of 40 quarters of paying social security tax from their earning qualify to receive DI benefits in the event of a disability. In 2002, 750,000 disabled workers were receiving an average of $834 a month in benefits.[2] Most of the disabled persons who qualified for income supports, qualified through SSI. In 2002, 6.8 million people were receiving SSI. For 55 percent of these recipients, it was their only source of income, and of those that do have other income, 35 percent receive their income from Social Security. Of the 6.8 million people who received SSI in 2002, 81 percent were disabled. The remainder were elderly and poor. Fifty-seven percent were adults (18-64) and 14% were children (see figure 9.1). Six out of 10 SSI participants were diagnosed with a mental disorder.

The average monthly SSI benefit in 2002 was $407, however, children received the highest benefit with an average payment of $428 (see figure 9.2). Slightly more than a million individuals received both SSI and DI in 2002. These numbers reflect only federal benefits. Some states also operate SSI programs, and disabled persons may be eligible for both state and federal benefits. Most (64%) received only federal benefits, while 32 percent received federal and state SSI benefits. State benefits tend to be considerably lower than federal benefits. State SSI programs are intended to supplement the federal benefit. A few (4%) received only state benefits (see figure 9.3). Recipients may qualify for state benefits but not federal benefits if the state's eligibility criteria are more generous than the federal criteria.[3] Despite their disabilities, 6% of SSI recipients also earned income in the work place in 2002.[4]

Figure 9.1: Composition of SSI Recipients by Eligibility and Age 2002

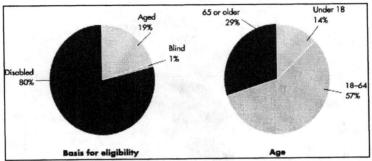

Source: Social Security Administration

Figure 9.2: Average Monthly Payment for Federally Administered SSI Benefits 2002

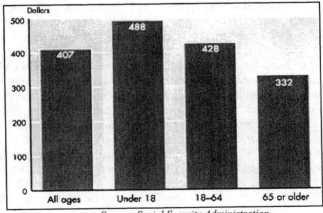

Source: Social Security Administration

159

Figure 9.3: Type of SSI Payments
2002

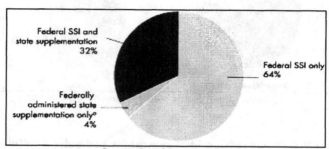

Source: Social Security Administration

When the SSI program began in 1974, there were 70,900 blind and disabled children receiving SSI. That number increased to 995,000 in 1996.[5] The welfare reform law in 1996 established a new definition of childhood disability, limiting SSI to children who meet a set of official conditions called the medical listings. While the law allowed a child's functioning to be considered in determining eligibility, the use of assessments of a child's functioning and references to maladaptive behavior were eliminated.[6] Because of these restrictions in eligibility criteria, the implementation of the welfare reform provisions resulted in close to 150,000 children losing their SSI benefits by 2000 when SSI was serving only 847,000 children. Child enrollment began to climb again in 2002 and SSI served 914,000 disabled children in that year. Children who were receiving SSI prior to the enactment of the new welfare law (Aug. 22, 1996) continued to be eligible for Medicaid if they lost their SSI benefits due to new disability definitions (see figure 9.4).[7]

Figure 9.4: Children Receiving SSI

Number of children under age 18 receiving SSI, selected years

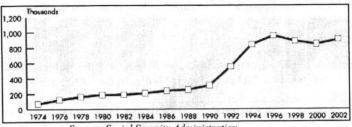

Source: Social Security Administration

Ticket-to-Work Medicaid Buy-Ins

Over 7 million individuals with disabilities rely on Medicaid for medical and supportive services. However, when working age individuals with disabilities increase their earnings, they risk losing health care coverage through Medicaid. In an effort to meet this challenge and minimize the risk of loss of health care coverage for disabled individuals who desired to work and increase their earnings, Congress passed the Ticket to Work and Work Incentives Improvement Act of 1999 (effective October 1, 2000). This legislation authorized states to raise their Medicaid income and asset eligibility limits for individuals with disabilities. State may require that working individuals with disabilities "buy in" to the program by sharing in the cost of their coverage. These state programs are referred to as Medicaid Buy-In programs. In December 2002, the GAO identified those states that had taken advantage of the new legislation and designed and implemented a Medicaid Buy-In program, and analyzed the characteristics of their programs, and the characteristics of those enrolled in the Medicaid Buy-In programs. As of December, 2002, 12 state had implemented Medicaid Buy-In programs. In order to capture more disabled individuals in the Medicaid safety net, states increased eligibility income and asset levels. Eligibility levels ranged from 100% of the Federal Poverty Level (FPL) (Wyoming) to no income limit (Minnesota). Most states set income limits at 200% of poverty threshold or greater. Connecticut's eligibility income is not connected to FPL. State required participants to buy into the program by charging premiums and co-payments for services (see table 9.2). Premiums ranged from $26 to $82 per month, and co-payments range from $.50 to $3.00 a visit. At the time of the study, 24,000 additional people had enrolled in Buy in programs. Most were low income earners making less than $800 per month.[8]

Table 9.2: Enrollment and Income Eligibility Characteristics of 12 States with Ticket to Work Medicaid Buy-In Programs

State	# Enrolled	Buy-In Start Date	Income Limit as % of FPL*
Missouri	8,461	July 2002	250%
Minnesota	6,178	July 2001	No Limit
Indiana	3,318	July 2002	350%
Connecticut	2,433	October 2000	$75,000
Pennsylvania	1,325	January 2002	250%
New Hampshire	968	February 2002	450%
New Jersey	551	February 2001	250% (earned) & 100% (unearned)
Kansas	489	July 2002	300%
Illinois	323	January 2002	200%
Washington	144	January 2002	220%
Arkansas	65	February 2001	250%
Wyoming	3	July 2002	100%

Source: U.S. General Accounting Office
* The FPL for an individual in 2002 was $8,860 annually.

The successes in expanding Medicaid and insuring more low-income disabled persons may be in jeopardy. The sluggish economy and rising unemployment have led to a rise in Medicaid enrollment at a time when states are trying to contain cost growth. For the first time in seven years, states slowed the growth of spending on Medicaid by three percent. The growth rate in FY2002 was 12.8 percent, and was down to 9.3 percent for FY2003. Cost containment strategies states have implemented included increasing co-payments for medical services, cuts in services, and tightening eligibility criteria. All 50 states and the District of Columbia implemented measures to control the cost of Medicaid during fiscal 2003 and all are planning additional action for fiscal 2004

According to the Kaiser survey[9], in fiscal 2004:

- 49 states plan to reduce or freeze rates on payments to Medicaid providers, such as physicians and inpatient hospital rates;
- 44 states will consider reducing prescription drug prices through preferred drug lists (PDLs);
- 20 states plan to reduce benefits to Medicaid patients – including restricting or eliminating dental coverage, vision coverage, doctor visits and home care; and,
- 18 states plan to change income standards for Medicaid eligibility and long-term care.[10]

President Bush's New Freedom Initiative

The New Freedom Initiative, announce in February 2001, is a nationwide effort to remove barriers to community living for people of all ages with disabilities and long-term illnesses. Departments throughout government have been directed to work in partnership with states to provider elderly and disabled persons with supports needed for full participation in community life. The initiative aims to put more disabled persons in the work force, and to transition people out of nursing homes and other institutional living settings to community living, when appropriate. President Bush has proposed to fund the New Freedom Initiative at $1.75 billion over a five year period. The funds will be used as grant funds to states to develop demonstration projects for meeting the initiatives objectives. Other funding focuses on demonstration projects for moving disabled children out of institutions and into community living. Funding initiatives include:

- "Money Follows the Individual" Rebalancing Demonstration – which will provide $1.75 billion over five years, with $350 million proposed for FY 2004. This five-year demonstration would assist states in developing and implementing a strategy to

163

"re-balance" their long term care systems so that there are more cost-effective choices between institutional and community options, including financing Medicaid services for individuals who transition from institutions to the community.

- New Freedom Initiative Demonstrations – will provide $220 million over five years, with $11 million proposed for FY 2004. This initiative would fund four demonstrations that promote home and community-based care alternatives. Two of the demonstrations provide respite care services for caregivers of adults with disabilities or long-term illness and children with substantial disabilities. Another demonstration provides community-based care alternatives for children who are currently residing in psychiatric residential treatment facilities. The President proposed these demonstrations for FY 2003.

- Spousal Exemption – provides $95 million over five years, with $16 million proposed for FY 2004. This proposal would continue Medicaid eligibility for spouses of disabled individuals who return to work. Under current law, individuals with disabilities might be discouraged from returning to work because the income they earn could jeopardize their spouse's Medicaid eligibility. This proposal would extend to the spouse the same Medicaid coverage protection now offered to the disabled worker.

Last year the President named his New Freedom Commission on Mental Health, and charged it with conducting a comprehensive study of the United States mental health service delivery system, including both private and public sector providers, and advising him on methods of improving the system. Secretary Thompson also created a new Office on Disability within HHS in 2002 to coordinate activities across the Department and serve as a focused contact point for disability issues.[11]

ENDNOTES

1. U.S. Census Bureau, *Disability Status: 2000 Census 2000 Brief,* Washington DC. Available at

http://www.census.gov/hhes/www/disable/disabstat2k/table1.ht ml Accessed September 28, 2003.

2. Social Security Administration, *SSI Annual Statistical Report, 2002,* Washington DC.

3. Social Security Administration, *Facts and Figures about Social Security,* Washington DC, 2003. Available at http://www.ssa.gov/policy/docs/chartbooks/fast_facts/2003/ff200 3.html#ssi   Accessed September 19, 2003.

4. Social Security Administration, *SSI Annual Statistical Report, 2002,* Washington DC.

5. Social Security Administration, *Facts and Figures about Social Security,* Washington DC, 2003. Available at http://www.ssa.gov/policy/docs/chartbooks/fast_facts/2003/ff200 3.html#ssi   Accessed September 19, 2003.

6. Children's Defense Fund, *Summary of the 1996 welfare law* (Public Law 104-193) Washington DC June 20, 2000 http://www.childrensdefense.org/fs_welflaw96.php#foodstamps Accessed September 25, 2003

7. Social Security Administration, *Facts and Figures about Social Security,* Washington DC, 2003. Available at http://www.ssa.gov/policy/docs/chartbooks/fast_facts/2003/ff200 3.html#ssi   Accessed September 19, 2003.

8. U.S. General Accounting Office, *Report to Congressional Committees Medicaid and Ticket to Work: States' Early Efforts to Cover Working Individuals with Disabilities,* GAO-03-587 (Washington DC: June, 2003). Available at www.gao.gov/cgi-bin/getrpt?GAO-03-587 Accessed September 7, 2003

9. The Kaiser Survey, as cited in Erin Madigan, *States Still Struggling To Control Medicaid Costs*, Stateline.org, (Washington DC: September 25, 2003. Available at http://www.stateline.org/story.do?storyId=326344 Accessed September 28, 2003

10. Erin Madigan, *States Still Struggling To Control Medicaid Costs*, Stateline.org, (Washington DC: September 25, 2003. Available at http://www.stateline.org/story.do?storyId=326344 Accessed September 28, 2003.

11. U. S. Department of Health and Human Services, *President will Propose $1.75 Billion Program to Help Transition Americans with Disabilities from Institutions to Community Living,*

(Washington DC: HHS Press Office) January 23, 2003.
http://cms.hhs.gov/newfreedom/nfi12303pr.asp

NOTES

NOTES

NOTES

NOTES

NOTES

NOTES

NOTES

NOTES